the handbook of
QUILTING

SALLY MILNER PUBLISHING

Welcome to the wonderful world of quilting

Initially used as a technique for making essential bedcovers, quiltmaking now has become an irresistible pastime for those captivated by quilts, both old and new. The quilts in this book capture something of the heritage inherent in quiltmaking – some using traditional blocks, others with a more contemporary feel. Once you have mastered the techniques, you too will delight in making these quilt treasures, which are sure to become your family's future heirlooms.

the handbook of
QUILTING

Contains all you need to know to ensure success every time.
- Step-by-step instructions
- Easy-to-follow diagrams
- Every quilt pictured in full color
- Full-sized templates and patterns
- Hand-pieced, machine-pieced and appliquéd quilts are all included
- Projects for all levels of ability

the handbook of *QUILTING*

contents

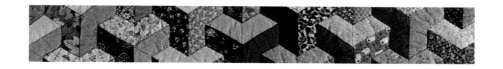

hand quilting

Long before the advent of the sewing machine, women were required and encouraged to stitch by hand. Today, hand-stitching remains a valued opportunity for self-expression and creativity, as well as an opportunity for quiet contemplation in an increasingly busy world.

The quilts in this section are made mostly by hand, employing methods used before the invention of the sewing machine and still favoured by many quiltmakers today. Although slower than machine-sewing, handwork is portable and enables the quilter to continue stitching while interacting with family and friends.

TEMPLATES

The making of accurate templates is one of the most important aspects of all pieced work.

For hand-piecing, templates are used to mark the sewing line on the fabric, not the cutting line. Templates for hand-piecing do not include seam allowances; these must be added when the piece is cut from the fabric.

MAKING TEMPLATES

Templates can be made from cardboard or from template plastic. The latter is preferable because you can draw directly onto the plastic and the edges do not become 'furry' from use. Furthermore, because the plastic is transparent, you can see how the piece will look when it is cut. (The situation with appliqué templates is a little different and that is covered on page 82.)

Begin by placing a sheet of template plastic over the appropriate template in the book or on the pattern sheet. Trace the templates onto the template plastic, using a ruler and fine permanent marker pen to mark the straight sides. Make sure you use a fine, not thick, line. For some quilts, even a tiny variation which is repeated in each template can create problems when you are putting the quilt together. It is a good idea to mark the corners of the pattern with a dot, then join the dots with a ruled straight line to ensure accuracy.

Cut out the plastic template using paper scissors or a rotary cutter, ruler and self-healing cutting mat. Cut just inside the marked line. Label each template with the name of the quilt, the template name and the grain line.

CUTTING THE FABRIC

Always cut borders before you cut the templates, then set them aside. It is very frustrating to find that you don't have sufficient length of fabric remaining to cut the borders in one piece.

Mark the fabric on the wrong side for hand-piecing, using a pencil (B, yellow or silver, depending on the fabric). For appliqué, mark the templates onto the right side of the fabric. Keep your pencils very sharp to ensure the lines are accurate.

Place the fabric face down on your work surface. A sandpaper board, which holds the fabric still while you work, is a great aid for accurate marking.

Position the templates on the fabric at least 15 mm (1/2 in) apart so that seam allowances can be added when

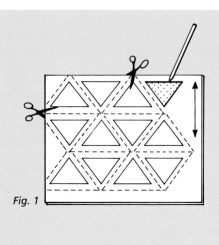

Fig. 1

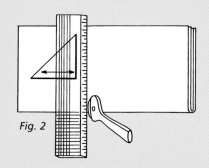

Fig. 2

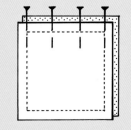

Fig. 3

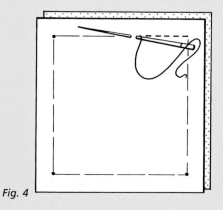

Fig. 4

cutting (Fig. 1). Make sure the grain line on the template is aligned with the grain line of the fabric, then draw carefully around the template. For fabrics which are non-directional, you can mark and cut several layers at once, using a rotary cutter or a sharp pair of scissors. If you are using scissors, pin the layers of fabric together to stop them from slipping about. For directional fabrics, always cut only one layer at a time.

Cut out each piece, allowing the 7.5 mm (1/4 in) seam allowance on all sides.

There is an interesting cutting method which combines the use of traditional marking techniques with the use of the rotary cutter. First mark the template on the wrong side of the fabric, without seam allowances, as usual. Place the ruler on the template so the 7.5 mm (1/4 in) marking is exactly on the edge of the template, then cut along the edge of the ruler with the rotary cutter (Fig. 2). This way you have perfect 7.5 mm (1/4 in) seam allowances, easy cutting and a marked sewing line.

HAND-PIECING
JOINING TEMPLATES

It is a good idea to lay out all the pieces for a block in their correct position, before you begin to sew them together. As with all piecing, whether by hand or by machine, the object is to join small units into bigger units and keep doing so until the block is completed.

Use an ordinary sewing thread in a matching or neutral colour and a betweens size 10 sewing needle.

Pin the shapes to be sewn together, with the right sides facing, placing pins at each corner and along the sewing lines (Fig. 3).

Thread the needle of your choice, knot the end of the thread and bring the needle up through the fabric exactly at the corner of the marked line. Beginning with a backstitch, sew along the sewing line, using a small running stitch – about eight stitches every 2.5 cm (1 in) (Fig. 4). It is important to check the back occasionally to make sure you are still sewing on the marked line. Keep your tension even – too loose and your work will pull apart at the seams; too tight and it will pucker along the seams. Finish at the other corner on the marked line, working several backstitches to secure the sewing. Remember, you do not sew into the seam allowances.

When the pieces are joined, press them carefully. More information about pressing follows.

JOINING ROWS

Usually the blocks are joined into rows, then the rows are joined (straight or diagonally) to complete the centre of the quilt top.

For joining rows, match the seam lines on the two rows, with the right sides together. Insert pins exactly at the corners of each piece and as close as possible to each seam. Sew up to the seam exactly as before, stopping just short of the seam. Work a firm backstitch on one side of the seam, pass the needle through the seam allowances so it emerges exactly on the corner of the sewing line (Fig. 5). Work another backstitch, then continue sewing to the end or to the next seam.

These days, many quiltmakers join rows of blocks by machine, even hand-pieced blocks.

PRESSING

Effective pressing is essential to making a successful quilt. Keep an iron and ironing board near your sewing machine and get into the habit of pressing every time you sew.

Pressing is just that – a firm pressure downwards with the iron. Do not pull and push the iron across the piece as this can cause it to become distorted.

Generally in quiltmaking seams are not pressed open, unless you are specifically instructed to do so. Seams are usually pressed in the direction of the darker fabric, preventing the shadow of the seam allowance showing through on the lighter fabric. An easy way to do this is to lay the piece on the ironing board with the darker fabric uppermost. Pick up the nearest corner of the darker piece and run the iron smoothly over the piece. This will automatically leave the pressed seam on the darker side.

It is not always possible to press the seams towards the darker fabric. For example, at a four-seam join, press the seam allowances all in the same direction (Fig. 6). This will ensure that the join in the centre lies as flat as possible. Where there is a set-in seam, press the seams all in the same direction (Fig. 7).

Not all pressing in quiltmaking is done with an iron. Seams can also be finger-pressed. This is quite effective with one hundred per cent cotton fabrics and is very useful if there isn't an iron handy. To finger-press, fold the seam allowance in the direction you wish it to go and draw your thumbnail firmly along the seam a couple of times (Fig. 8).

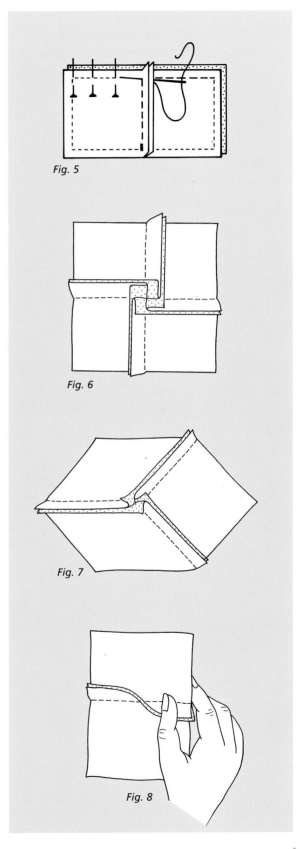

Fig. 5

Fig. 6

Fig. 7

Fig. 8

HAND-QUILTING

Quilting stitches perform the basic function of securing the layers of fabric and wadding. In that sense, hand-quilting has not only been around for a long time, but can be found in some unexpected places, such as in the padded, protective clothing worn by soldiers.

Quilting also has a decorative function and it is for this that we mainly value and appreciate quilting today. The small running stitches create wonderful patterns, many of which are hundreds of years old, and serve to highlight areas of the quilt. Often blocks and borders are outlined with quilting stitches.

THE QUILTING DESIGN

Many quilting designs are available to buy in the form of plastic stencils. Choose one that suits the style of your quilt and the size and shape of the area to be quilted. Some quilting patterns are given in this book. To use them you will need to cut your own stencil. Trace the design onto template plastic then, using a sharp scalpel, cut the design out of the plastic, taking care to leave a few 'bridges' between the cut-outs. The area you cut out should be quite fine, but wide enough for a pencil point to go through.

Another popular form of quilting is 'in-the-ditch'. This method is most favoured by machine-quilters. The stitches do not show up as well, so the effort of hand-quilting is not rewarded.

The simplest form of quilting is outline-quilting, where the stitches are worked approximately 7.5 mm (1/4 in) from the seam line (Fig. 9). Echo-quilting is also very popular. In this method, a particular motif is outlined with successive rows of quilting stitches which make it stand out quite dramatically (Fig. 10).

MARKING FOR QUILTING

The quilting design should be marked on the quilt top, before the quilt sandwich is assembled. Secure and cut off all threads and trim the raw edges on the quilt top. Press the top thoroughly because you will not be able to press it again.

To mark the quilting pattern, place the stencil on the right side of the quilt top and trace around it.

There are various marking tools available. Most quilters use some form of pencil, B or HB for light fabrics and yellow or silver for dark fabrics. In addition, there are washable fabric markers, usually blue, which can be used. If you plan to use one of these, test it on a small scrap of fabric, then wash it out to be sure that it is completely removed. Take great care not to heat-set the pen mark accidentally, such as by leaving your quilt too close to a heater or in the sun. Whichever marking method you use, apply it with a light touch. For hand-quilting, the lines need not be very dark at all. Some quilters avoid the problem altogether by using dressmaker's chalk. It is certainly easy to remove, but provides only very temporary markings for quilting.

When marking calico or another light-coloured fabric, the design can be traced. Draw the quilting design onto paper, and draw over it with a black felt-tip pen. Place the pattern under the fabric, then trace it using a B pencil and pressing very lightly. A light under a glass-topped table will facilitate the tracing.

Cross-hatching or grid-quilting (Figs. 11 and 12) can be marked on the quilt top, before assembling, but many quiltmakers do not do this. You can mark a small area at a time, using a long ruler and marking tools. A much simpler alternative is to use 7.5 mm (1/4 in) wide masking tape to define the rows for stitching. Do not leave the masking tape in place for an extended time as the adhesive can mark the fabric.

USING A HOOP

A hoop or frame is essential to maintain consistent tension throughout the quilting process. The quilt layers are held in place by the hoop, enabling you to work more quickly and evenly.

It is usual to begin quilting in the middle of the quilt and work out towards the edges. Place the inner circle of the hoop on a flat surface with the section of the quilt sandwich to be quilted over it. Loosen the screw on the outer loop, then put the outer hoop over the quilt and tighten the screw. If you have pin-basted, be careful to move any pins that might be caught in the hoop. The hoop defines the work area.

To quilt the borders, use a square frame or attach strips of plain fabric to the edges of the quilt top so the hoop can hold the edges taut.

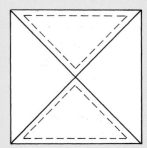

Fig. 9

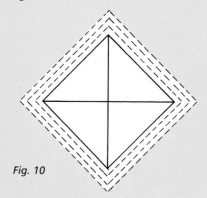

Fig. 10

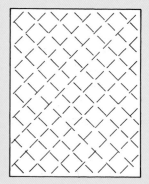

Fig. 11

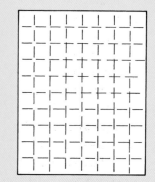

Fig. 12

BEGINNING TO QUILT

For hand-quilting a large quilt, which might take some time, it is generally preferable to baste the layers together. Some quilters, however, prefer to use 4 cm (1¹/₂ in) safety pins, placed very close together.

Assemble the quilt sandwich as instructed in fig. 13. Begin basting in the centre of the quilt. Thread your basting needle with a long thread of light-coloured cotton. Beginning at the centre, baste a diagonal line to each corner. Then complete a grid of horizontal and vertical lines, finishing with a row of basting around the edges (Fig. 14). The rows should be about 15 cm (6 in) apart. Complete the basting by rolling the quilt backing to the front, over the raw edges, and basting them in place to protect the raw edges during the quilting process. The more basting you do, the more secure will be the three layers.

THE QUILTING STITCH

For quilting, one hand is under the quilt, the sewing hand on the top (Fig. 15). Using a short betweens needle and quilting thread, thread the needle with a short length – approximately 45 cm (18 in) – of thread and tie a knot in the end.

Insert the needle through the quilt top and wadding, about 2.5 cm (1 in) away from where you wish to start quilting. Bring the needle up at the point where you will begin and, with a quick pull, pop the knot under the quilt top and bury it in the wadding. Now you are ready to begin quilting.

The hand-quilting stitch is a running stitch through the three layers of the quilt. While small stitches are highly prized, they are only achievable with practice. More importantly, keep the stitches an even size with equal spaces between them. Try to keep an even tension. As long as the effect is pleasing, don't be too disappointed if your stitches do not start off minute or if they are not exactly the same size on the top and bottom.

Position the thumb of your upper hand approximately 2.5 cm (1 in) ahead of the needle. Begin to take short running stitches through all three layers towards your thumb, rocking the needle up and down on the thimble (Fig. 15). The other hand is underneath the quilt. As soon as you feel the needle tip with the middle finger of your bottom hand, push the needle up, guiding its return. As soon as the tip is just visible, insert it again, just ahead of

where it emerged. Take three or four stitches at a time, working only with the tip of the needle, and pull the thread firmly to give that lovely sculptured look.

To complete a line of quilting, make a small knot near the last stitch, backstitch, then run the thread through the wadding. Pull the thread through again, leaving the knot embedded in the wadding. Cut the thread and allow the tail to slip back under the quilt top.

Some areas of the quilt may be difficult to quilt, particularly those where there are lots of seams. In these areas, some quilters employ a stab stitch, where only one stitch is made at a time, going straight down and coming straight up (Fig. 16). Alternatively, you can cheat a little and run the needle into the wadding then make a couple of stitches on the surface. The result will look like a continuous row of quilting on the front, but won't go all the way through the quilt sandwich.

The more quilting you do, the flatter your quilt will be. Try to keep the distribution of quilting even.

Do not leave your quilt in the hoop for long periods when you are not quilting. It may mark.

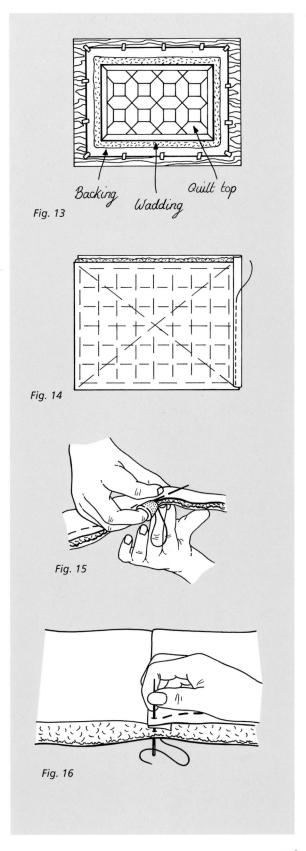

Fig. 13

Backing   Wadding   Quilt top

Fig. 14

Fig. 15

Fig. 16

BY JENNY SEARLE

Jenny found that her collection of blue and yellow fabrics was bulging out of its allotted space in her workroom, while the green and maroon collection languished for lack of attention. She decided to use some of her favourite blue and yellow fabrics to make this traditional quilt for her daughter.

The bold sunflower print of the border fabric is the perfect finishing touch.

This quilt is hand-pieced and hand-quilted.

FINISHED SIZE

Quilt: 193 cm (77 in) square
Block size: 30 cm (12 in) square
Total number of blocks: sixteen

FABRIC REQUIREMENTS

20 cm (8 in) of at least sixteen yellow fabrics (the more yellows you include, the scrappier the look)
Small pieces of terracotta-coloured fabric for the centre of the flowers (use as many different terracottas as you have in your scrap bag)
2 m (2¼ yd) of blue fabric for the background
1.6 m (1¾ yd) of navy-and-yellow print fabric for the sashing
70 cm (28 in) of terracotta-coloured fabric for the borders
2 m (2¼ yd) of a large sunflower print fabric for the wide border
2 m (2¼ yd) of blue fabric for the outer border and binding
4 m (4¼ yd) of fabric for the backing
200 cm (80 in) of wadding

OTHER REQUIREMENTS

Template plastic
Fineline permanent marker pen
Sandpaper board
Pencil, B
Matching sewing threads
Pair of compasses (optional)
Fabric scissors
Paper scissors
Thin cardboard
Quilting thread
Betweens needles, size 9 or 10
Safety pins (approximately 350)
Quilting hoop
Large square ruler
Rotary cutter and board
Glass-headed pins
Masking tape

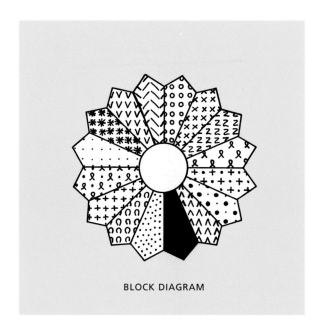

BLOCK DIAGRAM

MAKING TEMPLATES

See the templates on page 14. Note that the templates do not include seam allowances.

Trace templates A and B onto the template plastic, using the marker pen or the pencil. Mark the grain line on each template, then cut them out. It may be easier to draw your own circle with a 3 cm (1¼ in) radius than to try and accurately trace the one given. Cut sixteen of template B from the thin cardboard. Cut these out very carefully to give a perfect circle.

CUTTING

STEP ONE

Note: Measurements for the borders and bindings include seam allowances of 7.5 mm (¼ in).

• From the terracotta-coloured fabric, cut 4 cm (1½ in) wide strips across the width of the fabric.
• From the sunflower print fabric, cut 15.5 cm (6 in) wide strips down the length of the fabric.
• From the blue fabric for the border and binding, cut four 6.5 cm x 200 cm (2¼ in x 80 in) strips down the length of the fabric and four 9 cm x 200 cm (3½ in x 80 in) strips for the binding.

STEP TWO

From the blue background fabric and using the large square ruler, rotary cutter and board, cut out sixteen

sunflowers

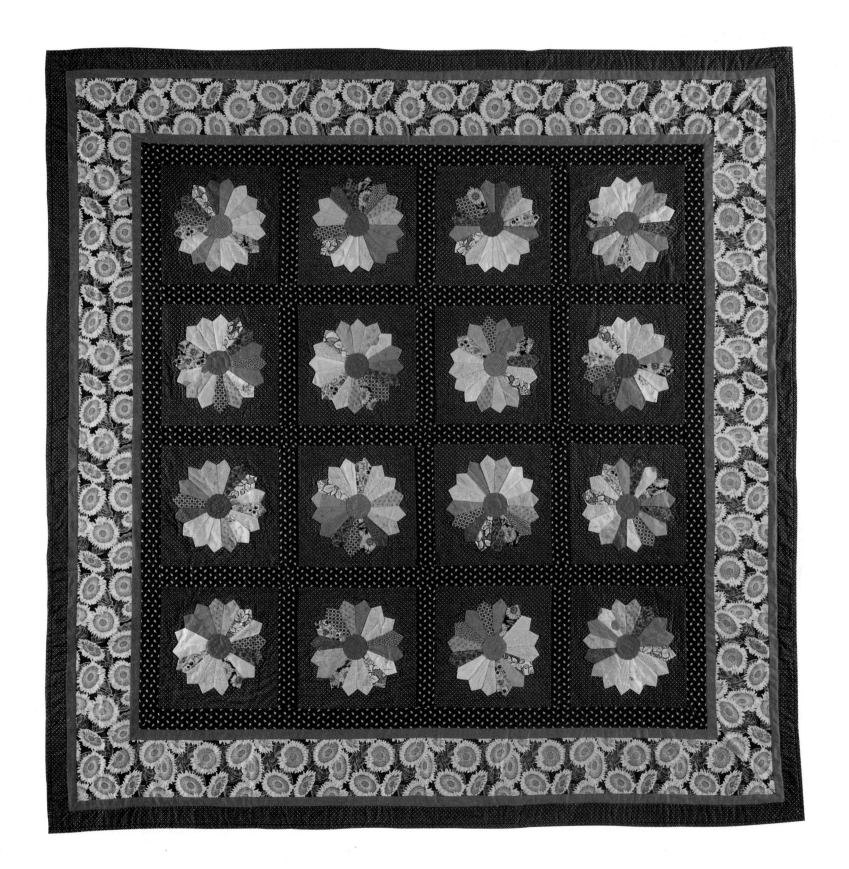

sunflowers

31.5 cm (12¹/2 in) squares. This measurement includes a 7.5 mm (¹/4 in) seam allowance. If you don't have a rotary cutter and square ruler, draft a 30 cm (12 in) square on thick cardboard and use this as a template to cut out the sixteen background squares. Trace carefully around the template, leaving space between them for seams. This pencil line will be your sewing line. Cut out each square approximately 7.5 mm (¹/4 in) from the sewing line.

STEP THREE

For each block, cut the following pieces:
• 16 of template A from a variety of yellow fabrics; and
• 1 of template B from the terracotta-coloured fabric. When cutting out the terracotta circles, leave a 1.5 cm (⁵/8 in) seam allowance outside the sewing line to enable the fabric to be basted to the cardboard.

STEP FOUR

For the sashing, cut the following pieces:
• four 6.5 cm x 155 cm (2¹/2 in x 62 in) pieces down the length of the fabric;
• three 6.5 cm x 139 cm (2¹/2 in x 56 in) pieces down the length of the fabric; and
• twelve 6.5 cm x 31.5 cm (2¹/2 in x 12¹/2 in) pieces for the short sashing pieces.

SEWING A PETAL

PIECING

STEP ONE

The steps for making the petals are shown in the picture on this page. Fold each petal over double, lengthwise, with the right sides together. Stitch across the top on the sewing line. Cut off the corner of the seam allowance nearest to the fold, then turn the petal to the right side. Push out the point neatly and press it flat. Make sixteen petals for each block.

STEP TWO

Slipstitch the sixteen petals together, arranging the colours randomly, or you could arrange the yellows from light to dark as Jenny has done.

STEP THREE

Baste a terracotta circle over a cardboard circle. Appliqué it in the centre of the pieced flower, using a terracotta thread and a small slipstitch. Remove the basting and take out the cardboard through the small hole in the centre back of the flower.

STEP FOUR

Find the centre of the background square by folding it into quarters and finger-pressing the folds. Centre the completed flower on the background square and secure it with pins. Appliqué the flower in place, using a yellow thread and a small slipstitch. Make sixteen blocks in the same way.

STEP FIVE

Join four blocks in a row, alternating them with small sashing strips. Join the rows, alternating them with the 139 cm (56 in) long sashing strips to form the pieced centre of the quilt. Attach the 155 cm (62 in) sashing strips around the pieced centre, mitring the corners.

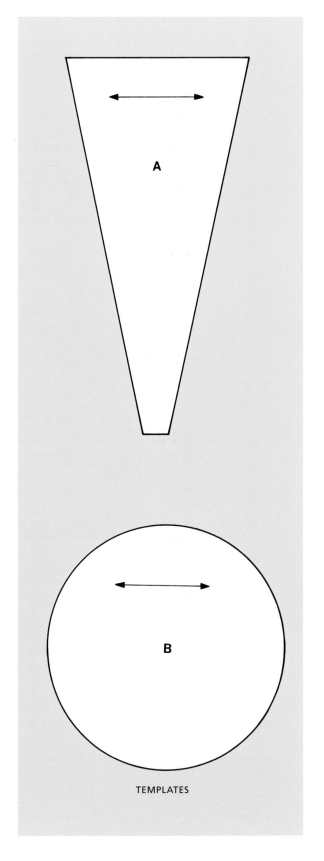

A

B

TEMPLATES

BORDERS

STEP ONE

Join the 4 cm (1$^1/_2$ in) wide strips of terracotta-coloured fabric to form four 160 cm (64 in) long pieces. Sew these to each side of the pieced top. Finish this narrow terracotta-coloured border with mitred corners.

STEP TWO

Measure the sides of the quilt. Trim each sunflower fabric strip to size. Sew a sunflower border to each side of the quilt top, mitring the corners.

STEP THREE

Measure the sides of the quilt. Join the remaining terracotta-coloured strips together to form four long strips. Attach one to each side of the quilt top, finishing them with mitred corners.

STEP FOUR

Sew on the blue borders to complete the quilt top, mitring the corners.

HINT

If you are using only sixteen different yellows you will need to cut out sixteen petals from each fabric. However, you may include as many different yellows as you like, even if they only occur once in the quilt. This adds to the interest and appeal of the quilt.

ASSEMBLING

STEP ONE

Cut the backing fabric in half to give two 2 m (2$^1/_4$ yd) lengths. Remove the selvages, then rejoin the pieces, lengthwise, to give a 200 cm x 220 cm (80 in x 88 in) backing piece. Trim 10 cm (4 in) from either side of this backing piece to make it 200 cm (80 in) square.

STEP TWO

Tape or pin the backing fabric face down on the work surface. Centre the wadding on top and the quilt top on top of that, face upwards. Smooth out each layer as it is put down. Keeping the three layers as flat as possible, pin them together at about 10 cm (4 in) intervals, using the safety pins.

QUILTING

STEP ONE

Hand- or machine-quilt around each block in-the-ditch. This will hold the quilt sandwich together while the hand-quilting is being completed.

STEP TWO

Hand-quilt as desired. Jenny has echo-quilted each flower and quilted a circle in each centre.

TO FINISH

STEP ONE

Carefully trim the wadding and the backing to the size of the quilt top. Press the binding strips over double, lengthwise. Find the centre of the binding strip and of the quilt sides by folding. Machine-stitch the binding to the right side of the quilt, matching the centres. Mitre the corners of the binding.

STEP TWO

Turn the folded edge of the binding to the back of the quilt and slipstitch it into place. Mitre the corners on the back and finish by hand.

STEP THREE

Label your quilt.

THE SUNFLOWER BLOCK

THREE MITRED BORDERS

BY SUE MANCHIP

Sue made twelve Inner City blocks in light, medium and dark green for a 'Block of the Quarter' competition and was lucky enough to win one hundred blocks. With these as her base, Sue decided to add to them to make a whole quilt.

This quilt depends for its effect on the enormous variety of fabrics used and the strict placement of the light, medium and dark greens.

This quilt is hand-pieced and hand-quilted.

FINISHED SIZE

Quilt: 145 cm x 210 cm (57$\frac{1}{2}$ in x 83$\frac{1}{4}$ in)

Block size: made up of three 3 cm (1$\frac{1}{4}$ in) hexagons

Total number of blocks: one hundred and twelve

FABRIC REQUIREMENTS

Scraps of green fabric in light, medium and dark tones

10 cm (4 in) of mid-green plain fabric

2.2 m (2$\frac{1}{2}$ yd) of dark green fabric for the borders and binding

3.2 m (3$\frac{5}{8}$ yd) of fabric for the backing

155 cm x 220 cm (61 in x 86$\frac{1}{2}$ in) of wadding

OTHER REQUIREMENTS

Template plastic

Fineline permanent marker pen

Sandpaper board

Pencil, B

Pencil for marking dark fabrics, silver or yellow

Matching sewing thread

Quilting thread, green

Fabric scissors

Glass-headed pins

Betweens needles, size 9 or 10

Long thin needle for basting

Quilting hoop

Safety pins

Masking tape

Firm paper or light cardboard

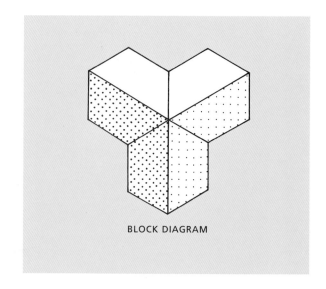

BLOCK DIAGRAM

MAKING TEMPLATES

See the templates on pages 18 and 19. Note that the templates do not include seam allowances. Add 7.5 mm (1/4 in) as you cut them out of the fabric.

Trace templates A, B, C and D onto the template plastic with the marker pen. Mark the grain line on the templates. Trace a second template B, turn it over and mark it Br, giving you the mirror image of template B.

CUTTING
STEP ONE

Place the fabric on the sandpaper board, wrong side up. With the grain lines matching, carefully trace two of template A from each scrap, noting that you will need two light, two medium and two dark half-hexagons for each complete block. Cut sufficient pieces for one hundred and twelve blocks. Pin together the two light, two medium and two dark half-hexagons that you have chosen for each block.

HINT

You may choose to cut out each block as you go, rather than cut them all out at the beginning, especially if friends happen to give you some of their treasured greens or, of course, you add to your own supply.

lucky me

STEP TWO

For the chevron border, cut the following pieces:

- cut one of template B and one of template Br from each of 72 fabrics (use as many different greens as you can);
- 8 of template C; and
- 4 of template D from the mid-green plain fabric.

STEP THREE

For the dark green borders, cut down the length of the fabric:

- two 11.5 cm x 144 cm (4$\frac{1}{2}$ in x 56$\frac{3}{4}$ in) strips for the inner borders;
- two 11.5 cm x 96 cm (4$\frac{1}{2}$ in x 38$\frac{1}{2}$ in) strips for the inner borders;
- two 18.5 cm x 180 cm (7$\frac{1}{4}$ in x 71 in) strips for the outer borders; and
- two 18.5 cm x 149 cm (7$\frac{1}{4}$ in x 59$\frac{1}{2}$) strips for the outer borders.

Note: seam allowances of 7.5 mm ($\frac{1}{4}$ in) are included in these measurements.

PIECING

STEP ONE

For each block, make three hexagons, one using a light and a dark A, one using a light A and a medium A, and one using a dark A and a medium A. Join them together as shown in the block diagram, keeping the darks on the left side, the mediums on the right side and the lights on the third side. Make one hundred and twelve blocks.

STEP TWO

Keeping the darks on the left side, sew the completed blocks together, forming the central section of the quilt top. This section is eight blocks wide and fourteen blocks long. To make this section rectangular, add partial blocks as required, keeping the pattern of darks on the left side. Use the photographs as a guide.

STEP THREE

Sew on the inner dark green border, mitring the corners.

CHEVRON BORDER

STEP ONE

Sew twenty-four different B shapes together to form a long strip. Sew the matching Br shapes cut from the same fabrics together to form a similar long strip. Sew the strips together, lengthwise, to form the chevron, matching shapes from the same fabric. Sew two C pieces to the end of the chevron strip. Continue in a similar manner to form the other half of the chevron border, reversing the chevron direction as shown in figure 1. Make two.

STEP TWO

For the short chevron border, use fourteen B and Br shapes before adding the two C pieces and reversing the chevron direction. Make two. Attach a mid-green square (D) to both ends of the short chevron border strips.

STEP THREE

Attach the chevron borders. Attach the dark green outer borders, mitring the corners. Use the quilt photograph on page 17 as a guide.

HINT

You may wish to join the hexagons using the English-piecing method (see page 144). Cut six half-hexagons from firm paper or light cardboard exactly the size of the template. Cut six half-hexagons from light, medium and dark fabric, as above, including at least a 15 mm ($\frac{1}{2}$ in) seam allowance. Wrap the fabric around the paper or cardboard and baste them into place. With the wrong sides together and carefully matching the corners, whipstitch two hexagons together, using a matching thread. Repeat for each hexagon keeping the light, medium and dark as indicated in the block diagram. Assemble the blocks, then join them to make the quilt top in a similar manner. Remove the paper or cardboard once the entire quilt is assembled.

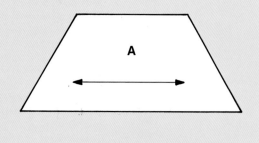

A

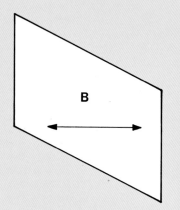

B

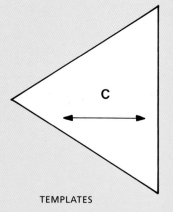

C

TEMPLATES

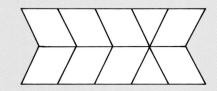

Fig. 1

ASSEMBLING

STEP ONE

Transfer the quilting design from template D to the small green squares.

STEP TWO

Cut the backing fabric into two equal 1.6 m (1¾ yd) lengths. Remove the selvages, then rejoin the pieces to form the complete backing, which is 1.6 m x 2.2 m (1¾ yd x 2½ yd).

STEP THREE

Pin or tape the backing fabric, face down, on the floor or a large table. Centre the wadding, then the quilt top (face up) in the centre of the backing fabric. Secure the layers of the quilt sandwich with basting or safety pins. Bring the excess backing fabric onto the front of the quilt and baste it over the raw edges to protect them during the quilting process.

QUILTING

Using the green quilting thread and quilting needle, quilt 'in-the-ditch' (along the seam lines) for each block in the pieced centre and each chevron. Quilt parallel lines, approximately 3 cm (1¼ in) apart, along the length of the dark green borders or quilt a pattern of your choice. Quilt the pattern into the green squares at the corners of the chevron border.

TO FINISH

STEP ONE

Carefully trim the wadding and the backing to the size of the quilt top. Cut 9 cm (3½ in) wide strips down the length of the fabric for the binding. You will need two pieces approximately 220 cm (86½ in) long and two pieces approximately 149 cm (58½ in) long. Press the strips over double.

STEP TWO

Machine-stitch the binding to the right side of the quilt, with the raw edges matching. Stitch the long sides first, then the top and bottom binding, allowing 15 mm (½ in) to extend beyond the quilt on both ends. Turn the folded edge of this binding to the back of the quilt and slipstitch all the binding in place. At each corner tuck in the excess binding to cover the raw edges.

STEP THREE

Label your quilt.

THE CORNER DETAIL

THE COMPLETED CHEVRON BORDER

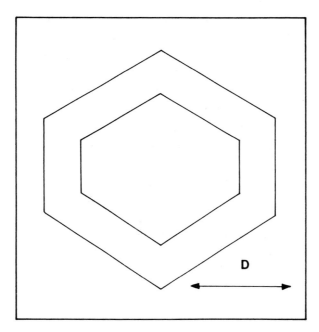

D

TEMPLATE

tribute to tralee

BY SUE MANCHIP

This was Sue's very first experience with friendship quilts. She chose the simple nine-patch of the Single Irish Chain pattern to evoke memories of friendship quilts of the past.

The quilting pattern Sue used features hearts, symbolising her friendship with the Mirrabooka Quilters.

This quilt is hand-pieced and hand-quilted.

FINISHED SIZE

Quilt: 192 cm x 234 cm (81 in x 99 in)

Block size: 21 cm (9 in) square

Total number of blocks: thirty-two pieced blocks and thirty-one plain blocks

Note: In this quilt, the conversion from metric to imperial measurements is not exact, as the nine-patch block is best attempted using a measurement divisible by three. If you are using imperial measurements you will need to draw a 3 in square for the template.

FABRIC REQUIREMENTS

10 cm (4 in) each of twenty different blue fabrics

Scraps of another twelve different blue fabrics

5 m (5$^1/2$ yd) of white fabric

2.1 m (2$^3/8$ yd) of blue print fabric for the border

5.3 m (5$^3/4$ yd) of fabric for the backing

1 m (1$^1/8$ yd) of blue fabric for the binding

202 cm x 244 cm (85$^1/2$ in x 103 in) of wadding

OTHER REQUIREMENTS

Template plastic

Heavy cardboard or rotary cutter and square ruler

Fineline permanent marker pen

Sandpaper board

Architect's tracing paper

Felt-tip pen

Large sheet of paper

Pencil, B

Matching sewing thread

Fabric scissors

Paper scissors

Quilting thread, white

Betweens needles, size 9 or 10

Long thin needle for basting, or safety pins (approximately 450)

Quilting hoop

Masking tape

Glass-headed pins

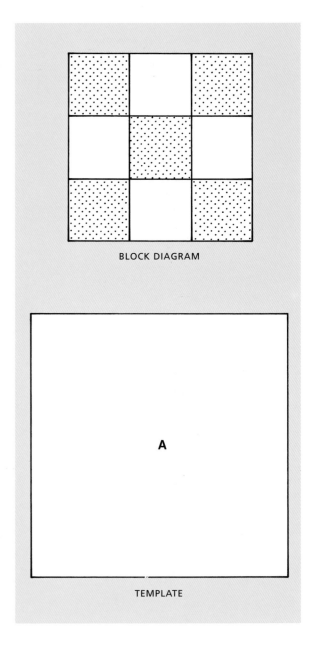

BLOCK DIAGRAM

A

TEMPLATE

MAKING TEMPLATES

See the template above and the quilting pattern on page 23. Note that the template does not include seam allowances. Add 7.5 mm ($^1/4$ in) when cutting them out of the fabric.

Trace the template onto the template plastic, using the marker pen or pencil. Mark the grain line on the template, then cut it out, using the paper scissors.

tribute to tralee

CUTTING

Note: Measurements for the borders include seam allowances plus an additional allowance of 4 cm (1^1/2 in) in length for adjustments.

STEP ONE

From the white fabric, cut two pieces 9 cm x 193 cm (3^1/2 in x 82^1/2 in) and two pieces 9 cm x 166 cm (3^1/2 in x 70 in) down the length of the fabric for the inner border.

STEP TWO

From the blue print fabric, cut two pieces 16.5 cm x 208 cm (6^1/2 in x 88^1/2 in) and two pieces 16.5 cm x 196 cm (6^1/2 in x 82^1/2 in) for the outer borders.

STEP THREE

For the plain squares, make a template from heavy cardboard that is a 21 cm (9 in) square. Mark thirty squares on the white fabric, leaving at least 15 mm (^{1}/2 in) between them. Cut out each square approximately 7.5 mm (^{1}/4 in) from the sewing line. Alternatively, cut thirty 22.5 cm (9^1/2 in) wide strips using a rotary cutter and square ruler, then cut the strips into squares. Note that seam allowances are included in these measurements for rotary cutting.

STEP FOUR

Cut out the following pieces:
- 128 of template A from the white fabric;
- 6 of template A from each of four blue fabrics;
- 10 of template A from each of ten blue fabrics;
- 9 of template A from each of six blue fabrics; and
- 1 of template A from each of the twelve blue scraps.

PIECING

STEP ONE

Twenty blocks are pieced using four white squares and five blue squares of the same blue fabric. Twelve blocks are pieced using four white squares and five different blues. The blues used in these twelve blocks should match the blue used in the diagonally adjoining block. This is apparent when you study the detail of the quilt. The blue centres in these blocks are those cut from scraps. Pin the pieces required for one block onto the large sheet of paper.

STEP TWO

Using the photographs and the block diagram as a guide, sew three squares together to form a row, then join three rows to complete the block.

STEP THREE

Join the completed blocks with the large white squares in rows in chequerboard fashion. Be careful to place the pieced squares so that the fabric used in the corners of diagonally adjacent blocks is the same.

INNER BORDER

Attach the long white border strips to both sides of the quilt top, then attach the remaining strips to the top and bottom of the quilt top, mitring the corners.

OUTER BORDER

Attach the 16.5 cm x 208 cm (6^1/2 in x 88^1/2 in) blue print strips to the sides of the quilt top. Attach the 16.5 cm x 196 cm (6^1/2 in x 82^1/2 in) blue print strips to the top and bottom of the quilt top, mitring the corners. While lengths of borders are given, it is always a good idea to measure your quilt top, measuring through the centre, and cut the borders to these lengths.

ASSEMBLING

STEP ONE

Trace the quilting patterns onto the architect's tracing paper, then outline the designs with the felt-tip pen. Place the large heart design under each large white square and trace the design onto the fabric using the pencil, pressing lightly. Trace the line of hearts onto the white borders in the same way.

STEP TWO

Cut the backing fabric in half to give two 2.4 m (2^7/8 yd) lengths. Remove the selvages, then rejoin the pieces to give the full-sized backing piece, which is 2.2 m x 2.4 m (2^1/2 yd x 2^7/8 yd).

STEP THREE

Pin or tape the backing fabric face down on the work surface. Centre the wadding on top, then the quilt top, face up, on top of that, smoothing each layer as it is put down. Keeping the three layers as flat as possible, pin them together at about 10 cm (4 in) intervals with the safety pins or baste the quilt sandwich.

QUILTING PATTERN

QUILTING

Using the white quilting thread, the betweens needles and the quilting hoop, hand-quilt the entire quilt in the marked patterns.

TO FINISH

STEP ONE

Carefully trim the wadding and the backing to the size of the quilt top. Cut the binding fabric into 9 cm (3$\frac{1}{2}$ in) wide strips across the width of the fabric. Join them to form two 238 cm (101 in) long strips and two 196 cm (83 in) long strips for the binding. Press each strip over double, with the wrong sides facing.

STEP TWO

Machine-stitch the binding to the long sides of the right side of the quilt, with the raw edges even. Turn the folded edge of the binding to the back of the quilt.

STEP THREE

Stitch the top and bottom binding, allowing at least 15 mm ($\frac{1}{2}$ in) to extend beyond the quilt on both sides. Turn the folded edge of this binding to the back of the quilt. Slipstitch all the binding in place. At each corner fold the excess fabric to cover the raw edges.

STEP FOUR

Label your quilt.

THE PLAIN SQUARES FEATURE BEAUTIFUL QUILTING

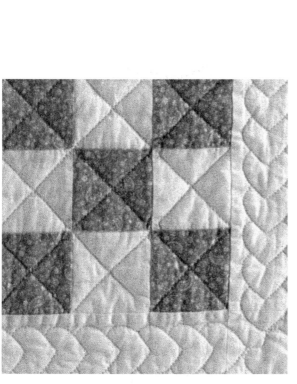

CLOSE-UP OF ONE BLOCK AND THE INNER BORDER
QUILTING PATTERN

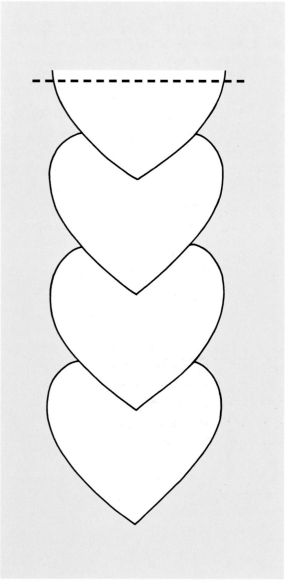

QUILTING PATTERN FOR THE INNER BORDER
NOTE THAT THIS PATTERN IS GIVEN IN TWO PARTS. TRACE THE PATTERN AS A WHOLE UNIT.

BY EVELYN SEYMOUR

Evelyn has always found yellow a difficult colour to include in her quilts. However, when she found a wonderful yellow fabric, she determined to rise to the challenge and make it work in a quilt.

This is a fascinating quilt design, where the gentle curves are an optical illusion created by perfectly straight lines. Evelyn chose the quilting design to emphasise the curves. This quilt is hand-pieced and hand-quilted.

FINISHED SIZE

Quilt: 100 cm x 132 cm (36^1/2 in x 49^1/2 in)

Block size: 12 cm (4^1/2 in) square

Total number of blocks: thirty-five

Note: The imperial measurements given for this quilt are not exact conversions but are based on using a 4^1/2 in block which is a convenient size to use.

FABRIC REQUIREMENTS

Large variety of soft-toned scraps

Large variety of brightly coloured scraps

70 cm (28 in) of white fabric for the triangles

50 cm (20 in) of blue fabric for the binding

1.4 m (1^5/8 yd) of fabric for the backing

1.5 m (1^2/3 yd) of yellow-and-blue print fabric for the border and pieced sashing

20 cm (8 in) of yellow spot fabric for the sashing

20 cm (8 in) of yellow swirl fabric for the centre of the Maltese cross

105 cm x 140 cm (41^1/2 in x 55 in) of wadding

OTHER REQUIREMENTS

Template plastic

Fineline permanent marker pen

Sandpaper board

Pencil, B

Matching sewing thread (a mid-grey is good when there are lots of fabrics to match)

Fabric scissors

Paper scissors

Quilting thread, cream

Glass-headed pins

Quilting hoop or frame

Betweens needles, size 9 or 10, for piecing and quilting

Safety pins (optional)

6 mm (1/4 in) wide masking tape

15 mm (1/2in) wide masking tape

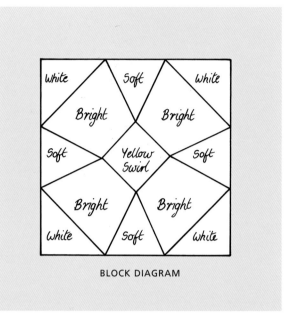

BLOCK DIAGRAM

MAKING TEMPLATES

See the templates on page 29. Note that the templates do not include seam allowances. Cut out each piece from fabric approximately 7.5 mm (1/4 in) from the sewing line.

Trace templates A, B, C, D, and E onto the template plastic, using the marker pen. Mark the grain line on each template, then cut them out carefully.

CUTTING

STEP ONE

From the yellow-and-blue print fabric, cut two 9.5 cm x 110 cm (3^1/2 in x 41 in) and two 9.5 cm x 142 cm (3^1/2 in x 53^1/2 in) pieces for the borders. Seam allowances of 7.5 mm (1/4 in) are included in these measurements, as is an added 10 cm (4 in) in the length to allow for mitred corners.

STEP TWO

For the sashing, cut the following pieces:

• 164 of template E from the yellow-and-blue fabric;

• 82 of template E from the soft-toned scraps; and

• 48 of template E from the yellow spot fabric for joining the sashing strips.

memories

memories

STEP THREE

For each block, cut the following pieces:
- 4 of template B from one of the brightly coloured scraps;
- 1 of template A from the yellow swirl fabric for the centre;
- 4 of template D from the white fabric; and
- 4 of template C from the soft-toned scraps, all different fabrics.

PIECING

STEP ONE

For each block, join a C triangle to either end of a B piece (Fig. 1). Join on a D triangle (Fig. 2). Make two sets. For the centre of the block, join two B pieces to either side of an A square, then add two D triangles, following the piecing diagram. Complete thirty-five blocks.

STEP TWO

Piece the sashing strips as shown in figure 3. Sew the sashing strips into rows, alternating them with a yellow spot square E and beginning and ending with a yellow spot square. Use five sashing strips and six squares for each sashing row. Make eight sashing rows.

STEP THREE

Alternating sashing strips and blocks, join five blocks and six sashing strips. Make seven rows.

STEP FOUR

Complete the pieced quilt top by sewing sashing rows and block rows together, alternately, using the photograph as a guide. Begin with a sashing row.

BORDERS

Attach the short border pieces to the ends of the pieced top, finishing sewing at the seam line. Attach the long border pieces to the sides of the quilt top, mitring the corners. Trim any excess fabric and press the mitre seam open. See page 151 for how to sew mitred corners.

ASSEMBLING

Pin or tape the backing fabric face down on the work surface. Centre the wadding on top and the pieced top on top of that, face upwards. Smooth out each layer as you put it down. When all the layers are perfectly flat, baste them together (or secure them with safety pins). Roll the excess backing to the front of the quilt and baste it in place to protect the edges during quilting.

QUILTING

Using the quilting thread and hoop or frame, hand-quilt the entire quilt following the guidelines shown in the quilting pattern diagram, or use a design of your own choosing. Use the 7.5 mm (¼ in) wide masking tape to mark out the design, The border is quilted, following the pattern in the fabric.

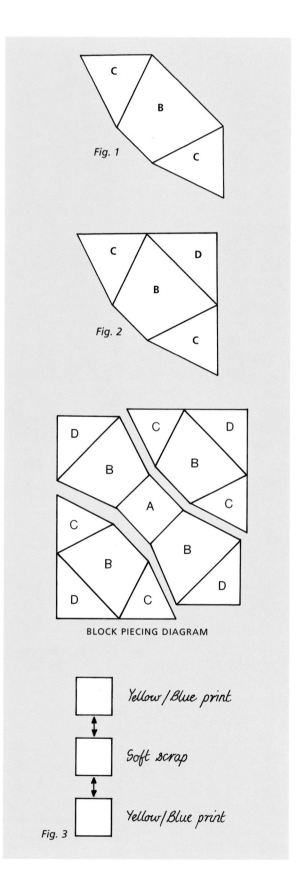

Fig. 1

Fig. 2

BLOCK PIECING DIAGRAM

Yellow / Blue print

Soft scrap

Yellow / Blue print

Fig. 3

TO FINISH

STEP ONE

Carefully trim the wadding and backing to the size of the quilt top. Cut the binding fabric into 9 cm (3^1/$_2$ in) wide strips across the width of the fabric. Join the strips to form two 140 cm (55 in) and two 108 cm (42^1/$_2$ in) lengths. Press the strips over double.

STEP TWO

Find the centre of the binding strips and the quilt sides by folding. Machine-stitch the strips to the right side of the quilt with the raw edges even, matching the centres. Attach the short binding to the top and bottom first, then attach the long binding strips to the sides of the quilt, mitring the corners. Turn the binding to the back of the quilt and slipstitch it into place.

STEP THREE

Label your quilt.

A PIECED BLOCK

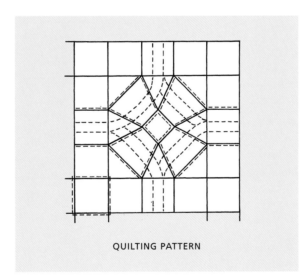

QUILTING PATTERN

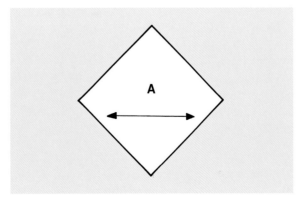

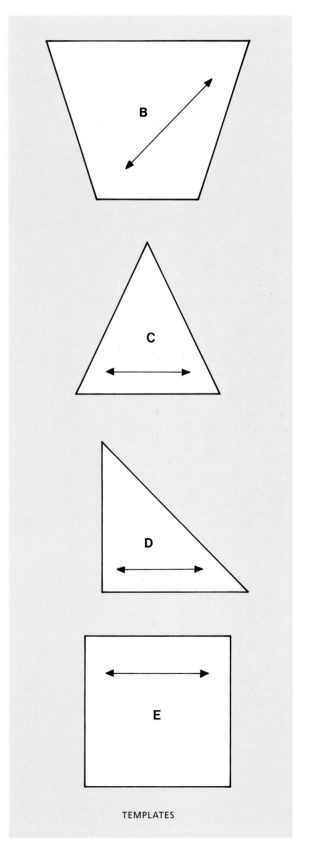

TEMPLATES

hearts & flowers

BY ROS STINSON

Ros used all her favourite pink and blue print fabrics to make a pretty quilt for her niece Jessica, who always enjoys sleeping under a quilt when she comes to stay. Jessica loves the pink and blue hearts.

The selection of fabrics allows the quilt to be 'quietly scrappy' while the two different quilted grids enhance the design.

Piecing the blocks for this quilt requires a little extra care as there are a few set-in seams to deal with.

This quilt is hand-pieced and hand-quilted.

FINISHED SIZE

Quilt: 160 cm x 200 cm (64 in x 80 in)
Block size: 40 cm (16 in) square
Total number of blocks: twelve

FABRIC REQUIREMENTS

20 cm (8 in) each of fifteen medium-blue fabrics, fifteen medium-pink fabrics and fifteen light blue/pink fabrics

4 m (4$\frac{1}{2}$ yd) of white fabric

2 m (2$\frac{1}{4}$ yd) of blue-and-white fabric for the outer border

1.9 m (2$\frac{1}{8}$ yd) of blue fabric for the inner border

4.4 m (4$\frac{7}{8}$ yd) of pink fabric for the binding and the backing (a light colour or white is best to avoid any show-through)

170 cm x 210 cm (68 in x 84 in) of wadding

OTHER REQUIREMENTS

Template plastic
Fineline permanent marker pen
Sandpaper board
Thin cardboard for appliqué
Pencil, B
Matching sewing thread
Quilting thread, white
Fabric scissors
Paper scissors
Glass-headed pins
Long thin needle for basting
Quilting hoop
Betweens needles, size 9 or 10, for piecing and quilting
7.5 mm ($\frac{1}{4}$ in) wide masking tape
Spray starch
Craft knife
Masking tape

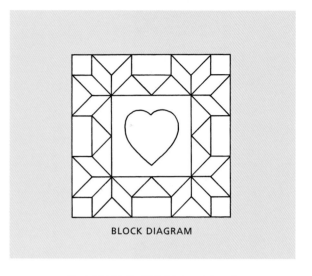

BLOCK DIAGRAM

MAKING TEMPLATES

See the templates and quilting patterns on pages 33 and 35 and the inner border quilting pattern on page 35. Note that the templates do not include seam allowances.

Using the marker pen, trace the templates A, B, C, D, E, F and G onto the template plastic. Trace template B a second time, cut it out, turn it over and mark it Br. Mark the grain line on each template. Cut out each template carefully from the plastic.

CUTTING

Note: The measurements for the borders and bindings include 7.5 mm ($\frac{1}{4}$ in) seam allowances. While lengths of borders are given, it is always a good idea to measure your quilt through the centre and cut the borders to those lengths.

STEP ONE

From the blue inner border fabric, cut two 9.5 cm x 146 cm (3$\frac{3}{4}$ in x 58 in) pieces and two 9.5 cm x 182 cm (3$\frac{3}{4}$ in x 73 in) pieces. Use the remainder as one of the blue fabrics for the blocks.

STEP TWO

From the blue-and-white print fabric for the outer border, cut two pieces 13.5 cm x 210 cm (5$\frac{1}{4}$ in x 84 in) and two pieces 13.5 cm x 170 cm (5$\frac{1}{4}$ in x 67 in) down the length of the fabric. Use the remaining fabric for one of the blue fabrics in the blocks.

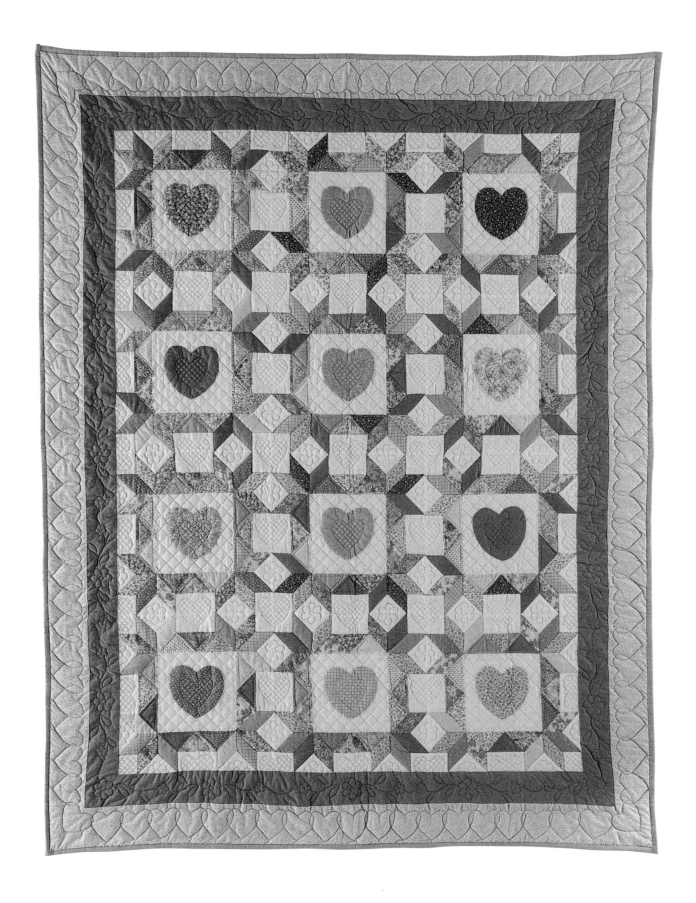

hearts & flowers

STEP THREE

From the pink fabric, cut eight 9 cm x 110 cm (3$\frac{1}{2}$ in x 44 in) pieces across the width of the fabric for the binding. The remaining piece is for the backing.

STEP FOUR

From the white fabric, cut the following pieces:
- 48 of template D;
- 96 of template C;
- 48 of template A; and
- 12 of template E.

STEP FIVE

Place the templates on the wrong side of the fabrics and draw around them with the pencil. This pencil line will be your sewing line. When marking fabric for the blocks, leave space between each shape to allow for seams. Cut out each piece approximately 7.5 mm ($\frac{1}{4}$ in) from the sewing line.

For each block you will need four D, eight C, four A and one E in white; four B from each of two blue, pink or light fabrics; four Br from each of two blue, pink or light fabrics; twelve C in assorted fabrics, different from those already used for the block; and one F using pink or blue fabric. Mark the sewing line on the right side of the fabric for F and allow 15 mm ($\frac{1}{2}$ in) for seam allowances.

HINT

You may wish to cut out all the white pieces first and only cut out the patterned pieces when you are ready to start a new block. That way you can make sure there is a balance in the use of the pink and blue fabrics.

APPLIQUE
STEP ONE

Cut out one F from the thin cardboard. Attach the fabric F to the cardboard by turning the seam allowance over the cardboard and basting it in place. Spray with a little starch, press, then remove the cardboard. Because this is a large piece to appliqué, you may want to dispense with the cardboard template and simply turn under and baste the seam allowance to the back. Cut the central V almost to the sewing line to facilitate either method.

STEP TWO

Find the centre of the large white square E by folding it into quarters. Finger-press the folds. Fold the heart in half vertically to find the centre. Appliqué the heart to the white square, matching the centre lines and using blue or pink thread as appropriate.

PIECING
STEP ONE

For each block, join eight B diamonds into pairs (Fig. 1). Join two more B diamonds to each pair (Fig. 2). Join an A square and two C triangles to each set to form the corners of the block (Fig. 3).

STEP TWO

Join twelve C triangles into groups of three (Fig. 4). Join a D rectangle to the set (Fig. 5).

STEP THREE

Join the four sets made in step 2 to the sides of the white square with the heart appliqué, then join on the four corner sets to complete the block, referring to the block piecing diagram. Make twelve blocks.

STEP FOUR

Sew the blocks together in three rows of four blocks each to form the centre of the quilt.

INNER BORDER

Find the centre of the border strips and of the sides of the pieced top by folding. Using the inner border strips already cut from the blue fabric and matching centres, attach the short strips to the top and bottom of the quilt, then attach the longer strips to the sides of the quilt top. Mitre the corners. Trim the seams and press.

OUTER BORDER

Using the blue-and-white border strips already cut and matching centres, sew the short strips to the top and bottom of the quilt, then attach the long strips to the sides. Mitre the corners. Trim the seams and press.

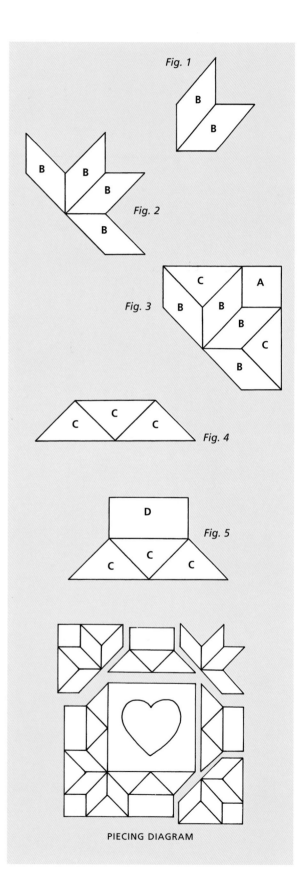

PIECING DIAGRAM

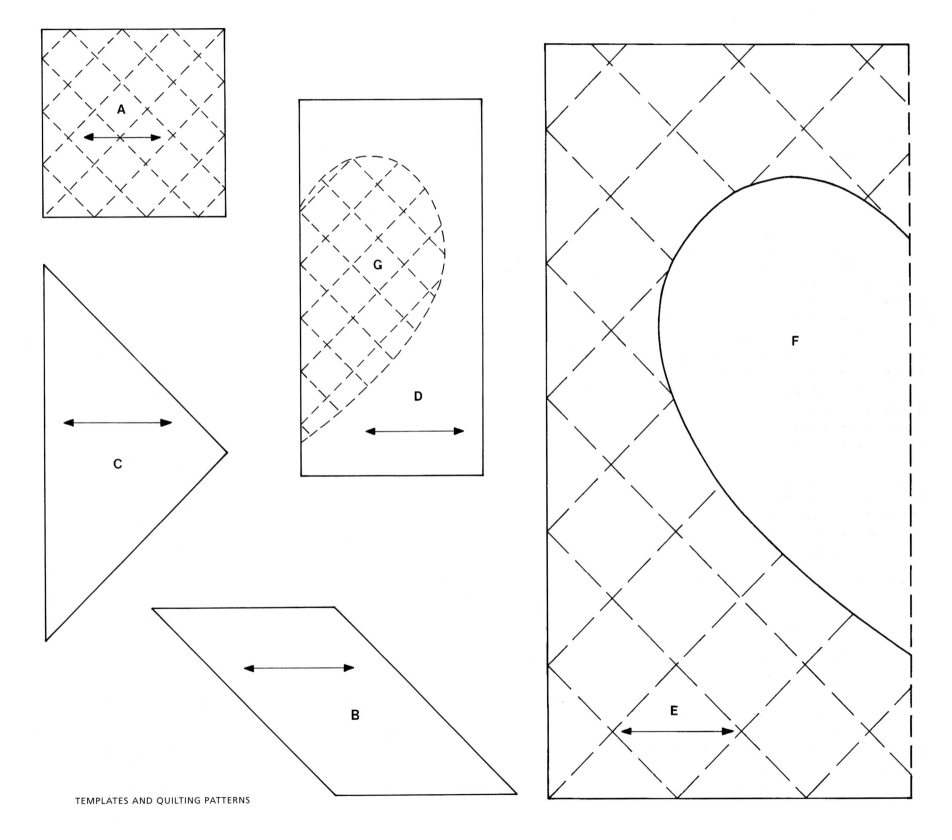

A

C

G

D

B

E

F

TEMPLATES AND QUILTING PATTERNS

ASSEMBLING

STEP ONE

Cut the remaining pink backing fabric into two pieces, each approximately 170 cm (68 in) long. Remove the selvages, then rejoin the pieces to form a backing that is 170 cm x 220 cm (68 in x 88 in).

STEP TWO

Following the quilting patterns indicated on the templates, mark the quilt top, using the pencil, or you can use your own pattern, if you prefer. To make the cross-hatching easier, cut strips from the template plastic, 1 cm (3/8 in) and 2.5 cm (1 in) wide and approximately 20 cm (8 in) long. Use these to mark the cross-hatching: the large square with 2.5 cm (1 in) cross-hatching and the small square and heart with 1 cm (3/8 in) cross-hatching.

STEP THREE

Mark the small heart quilting pattern onto the appliqué heart and the white square. The same pattern is also overlapped on the outer border. Placement of the design is clearly shown in the photograph of the quilt.

STEP FOUR

Trace the inner border quilting pattern onto the template plastic and make your own stencil using the craft knife. Cut along the lines, making a cut wide enough for a pencil to fit. The flower in this design is also used in the small white squares and white triangles in the block. Again, refer to the photographs for a guide.

STEP FIVE

Pin or tape the backing fabric face down on a table or on the floor. Centre the wadding on top, then the quilt top on top of that, face upwards. Smooth out each layer as it is put down. When all the layers are perfectly flat, baste them together, rolling the excess backing onto the front of the quilt and basting it over the raw edges to protect them during quilting.

QUILTING

Using the white quilting thread, quilting needle and hoop, hand-quilt the entire quilt, beginning at the centre and working out towards the edges.

TO FINISH

STEP ONE

Carefully trim the wadding and the backing to the size of the quilt top. Join the pink binding strips, already cut, to form two strips 204 cm (81 in) and two strips 164 cm (65 in) long. Press the strips over double. Find the centres of the quilt and of the binding, as for the borders. Machine-stitch the binding to the long sides of the right side of the quilt, with the raw edges even and the centres matching. Turn the folded edge of the binding to the wrong side of the quilt.

STEP TWO

Stitch the remaining strips to the top and bottom. Note that there is at least 15 mm (1/2 in) overhang at either end of the binding strips. Turn this binding to the back of the quilt and slipstitch all the binding in place, folding in the excess binding to cover the raw edges.

STEP THREE

Label your quilt.

QUILTING PATTERN

A QUILTED BLOCK, SHOWING THE DIFFERENT QUILTING PATTERNS

INNER BORDER QUILTING PATTERN

BY KAREN FAIL

Karen loves the look of Amish quilts and this miniature version of the 'Basket Quilt' allowed her to experiment with the Amish palette, without the work of a large quilt.

She has used two purples as the backdrop for the mini-baskets, contriving the look so often achieved naturally by the Amish. The mistake in the bright pink basket is deliberate, as the Amish say 'only God is perfect'.

This quilt is hand-pieced and hand-quilted.

FINISHED SIZE

Quilt: 37 cm x 45 cm (14$^1/2$ in x 17$^3/4$ in)
Block size: 6 cm (2$^3/8$ in) square
Total number of blocks: twelve

FABRIC REQUIREMENTS

Twelve different scraps of plain strong colours, one of these a lime green
10 cm (4 in) of two different shades of light and dark purple fabric
10 cm (4 in) of aqua fabric for the background in the blocks
25 cm (10 in) of black fabric
15 cm (4 in) of blue fabric for the outer border
40 cm x 50 cm (16 in x 20 in) of thin wadding
40 cm x 50 cm (16 in x 20 in) of fabric for the backing

OTHER REQUIREMENTS

Template plastic
Fineline permanent marker pen
Sandpaper board
Chalk dispenser
Pencil, B
Ruler
Pencil for marking dark fabrics, silver or yellow
Small plastic bags
Matching sewing thread
Quilting thread, black
Fabric scissors
Paper scissors
Glass-headed pins
Betweens needles, size 9 or 10
Long thin needle for basting
Craft knife
Paper and a glue stick (optional)

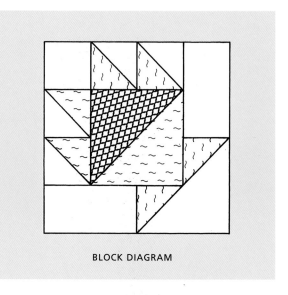

BLOCK DIAGRAM

MAKING TEMPLATES

See the templates and the quilting pattern on page 40. Note that the templates do not include seam allowances. Add 7.5 mm ($^1/4$ in) when cutting them out of fabric.

Trace the templates A, B, C, D, E, F, G, H and I onto the template plastic. Although cardboard is often used as an alternative to plastic for templates, it is essential to use template plastic for this quilt because the templates are so tiny. Mark the grain line on each one, then carefully cut out the templates.

CUTTING

STEP ONE

Note: Measurements for the borders and binding include 7.5 mm ($^1/4$ in) seam allowances.

From the black fabric, cut the following pieces:
• two 2.5 cm (1 in) wide strips across the width of the fabric, for the inner border; and
• two 6.3 cm (2$^3/8$ in) wide strips from the black fabric for the binding.

STEP TWO

From the blue fabric, cut two 5 cm (1$^7/8$ in) wide strips across the width of the fabric for the outer border.

STEP THREE

Place the scrap fabrics wrong side up on the sandpaper board. With the grain lines matching, carefully trace

amish baskets

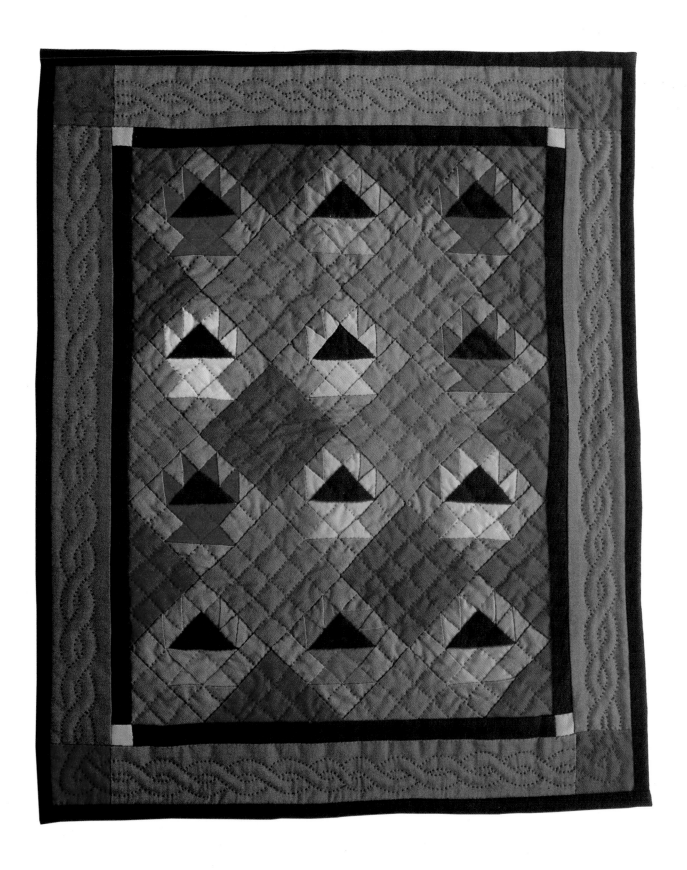

amish baskets

around the required number of templates for each fabric, leaving space between each shape to allow for seams. This pencil line will be your sewing line. Cut out each piece approximately 7.5 mm (1/4 in) from the sewing line.

Cut out the following pieces:

From the dark purple fabric:
- 8 of template A;
- 3 of template B;
- 2 of template C; and
- 4 of template I.

From the light purple fabric:
- 2 of template A;
- 1 of template B; and
- 4 of template C.

From the aqua fabric:
- 48 of template D;
- 12 of template E;
- 24 of template F; and
- 12 of template G.

From each of twelve different plains for the blocks:
- 6 of template D; and
- 1 of template E.

From the black fabric:
- 12 of template E.

From the lime green fabric:
- 4 of template H.

STEP FOUR

Assemble the pieces for each block, and place them in separate plastic bags.

HINT

The templates for the miniature Amish baskets are very small. As an alternative to cutting plastic templates and tracing them onto fabric, you could cut out paper templates and temporarily glue them to the fabric with a glue stick. Leave them in place until the block is sewn together, then remove them.

PIECING

STEP ONE

For each block, join a large black A triangle to a large coloured A triangle (Fig. 1).

STEP TWO

Sew a coloured D triangle to an aqua D triangle to make a square. Sew two of these squares together to make the set shown in figure 2. Make two. Sew an aqua square I to one end of one of these sets (Fig. 3).

STEP THREE

Sew the sets of small pieced squares, made in step 2, to the square made in step 1 (Fig. 4).

STEP FOUR

Sew a small coloured E triangle to one end of an aqua F. Make two, noting that they are mirror-reversed (Fig. 5). Sew these to the set made in step 3 (Fig. 5). Then, add an aqua triangle E to complete the block. Make twelve blocks, using a different plain fabric for each one. Notice the deliberate mistake in the centre bottom row.

STEP FIVE

Arrange the pieced blocks in diagonal rows with a light or dark purple A triangle at the ends of the rows to square them up. Join the rows, adding a light or dark purple B triangle at the four corners to complete the centre of the quilt top. Refer to the quilt photograph and the quilt diagram. It is important to carefully match the seams between the blocks.

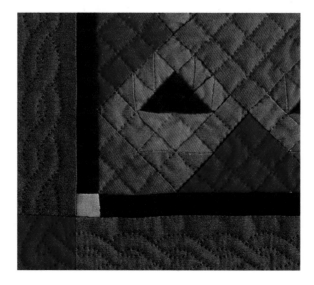

RIGHT: THE NARROW BORDER ADDS
SPARKLE TO THE QUILT

Fig. 1

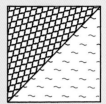

Fig. 2

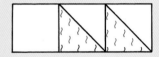

Fig. 3

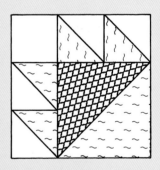

Fig. 4

INNER BORDER

STEP ONE

Cut one 2.5 cm (1 in) wide strip of black fabric into two lengths, 38 cm (15¼ in) long. Attach these strips to opposite sides of the quilt top. Trim.

STEP TWO

Measure the quilt top between the attached black strips. Use this measurement, plus 15 mm (½ in), to cut the remaining 2.5 cm (1 in) wide strip of black fabric into two pieces. Attach an H square of light green fabric to both ends of each strip, then attach a strip to the top and bottom of the quilt top, making sure that the small green square sits exactly in the corner.

OUTER BORDER

STEP ONE

Cut one of the 5 cm (1⅞ in) wide blue strips into two lengths, 42 cm (16½ in). Attach the strips to opposite sides of the quilt top. Trim.

STEP TWO

Measure the quilt top between the blue strips. Use this measurement, plus seam allowances of 15 mm (½ in) to cut the remaining 5 cm (1⅞ in) wide strip of blue fabric into two pieces. Attach one of the G squares of purple to each end of the blue strips. Stitch these strips to the top and bottom of the quilt top.

ASSEMBLING

STEP ONE

Using the marker pen, trace the quilting pattern onto the template plastic. Cut it out using the craft knife, being careful to remove the inner sections. The spaces should be quite narrow, but big enough for the point of a pencil to go through.

STEP TWO

Using the pencil and ruler, mark the quilt top with diagonal grid lines 1.5 cm (⅝ in) apart. Using the stencil, mark the quilting design along the border, beginning at the corners and working towards the middle, slightly reducing the centre loop.

STEP THREE

Lay the backing fabric face down with the wadding on top and the quilt top, on top of that, face up, smoothing out each layer as it is put down. Pin the layers together with the glass-headed pins, then baste the layers together, finishing by basting around the outside edge of the quilt.

QUILTING

Using the black quilting thread and a quilting needle, hand-quilt the entire quilt. A hoop is not required because of the small size of the quilt. For tips on hand-quilting see pages 10 and 11.

TO FINISH

STEP ONE

Carefully trim the wadding and the backing to the size of the quilt top.

STEP TWO

Cut two 49 cm (19 in) and two 41 cm (16⅜ in) strips from the black binding strip. Press the strips over double. Machine-stitch the binding to the right side of the quilt with the raw edges even. Stitch the long sides first, then turn the folded edge of the binding to the wrong side of the quilt.

STEP THREE

Stitch the top and bottom bindings. Trim, allowing 15 mm (½ in) to extend beyond the quilt on both ends. Turn the folded edge of this binding to the back of the quilt. On the back, slipstitch all the binding in place, folding the excess binding to cover the raw edges.

STEP FOUR

Label your quilt.

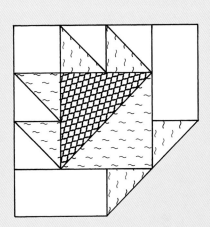

Fig. 5

QUILT DIAGRAM

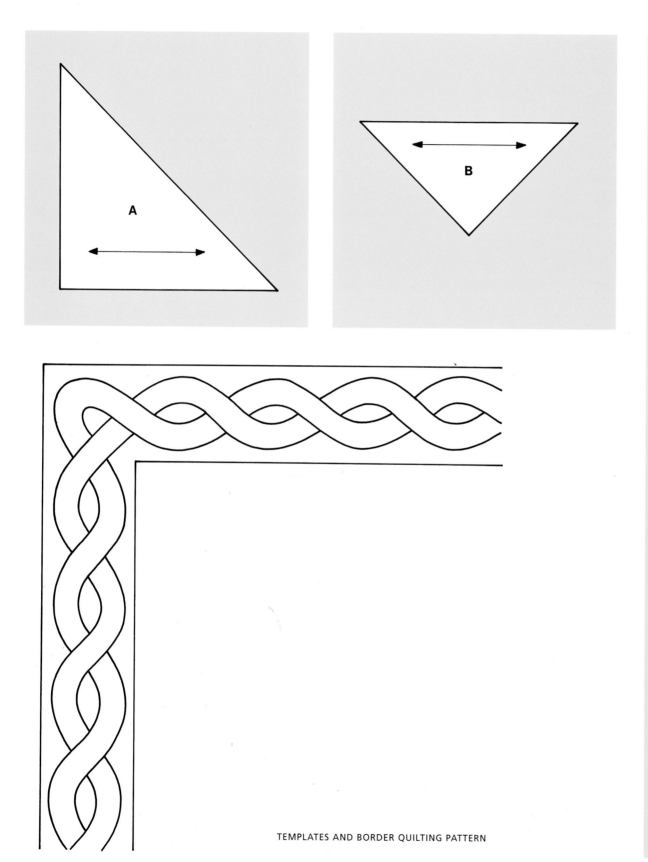

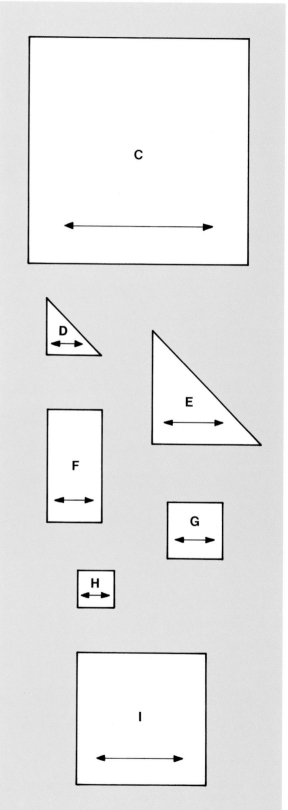

TEMPLATES AND BORDER QUILTING PATTERN

BY LEA LANE

'I like the idea of using small scraps which have little obvious value and creating a beautiful quilt, just as so many have done before me' says Lea.

To many people, scrappy quilts represent the traditions of quiltmaking. With so little fabric available, any textile was treasured. Even tiny scraps were incorporated into wonderful patterns by our enterprising ancestors. Lea's quilt is created in that tradition.

This quilt is hand-pieced and hand-quilted.

FINISHED SIZE

Quilt: 150 cm x 230 cm (60 in x 92 in)
Block size: 20 cm (8 in) square
Total number of blocks: sixty

FABRIC REQUIREMENTS

3.2 m (3^1/$_2$ yd) of yellow fabric
Sixty large scraps of dark fabrics
Smaller scraps of sixty medium and sixty light fabrics
2.4 m (2^2/$_3$ yd) of a large print fabric for the border
4.8 m (5^1/$_3$ yd) of fabric for the backing
155 cm x 235 cm (61^1/$_2$ in x 94 in) of wadding

OTHER REQUIREMENTS

Template plastic
Fineline permanent marker pen
Sandpaper board
Large sheet of paper
Pencil, B
Pencil for marking dark fabrics, silver or yellow
Matching sewing thread (mid-grey will blend with most fabrics)
Quilting thread, cream
Fabric scissors
Paper scissors
Glass-headed pins
Betweens needles, size 9 or 10
Long thin needle for basting or 4 cm (1^1/$_2$ in) safety pins
7.5 mm (^{1}/$_4$ in) wide masking tape
Masking tape
Quilting hoop, approximately 45 cm (18 in)

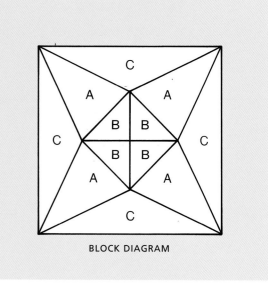

BLOCK DIAGRAM

A PIECED BLOCK SHOWING THE QUILTING DESIGN

*world
without end*

world without end

MAKING TEMPLATES

See the templates on page 45. Note that the templates do not include seam allowances. Add 7.5 mm (¼ in) when cutting them from fabric.

Using the marker pen, trace templates A, B, and C onto the template plastic. Mark the grain line on each one, then cut them out carefully.

CUTTING
STEP ONE

Note: Measurements for borders include a seam allowance of 7.5 mm (¼ in) and an additional 5 cm (2 in) on both ends for the mitre. While lengths are given, it is always a good idea to measure your quilt through the centre and cut the borders to those lengths.

From the yellow fabric cut two pieces 6.5 cm x 220 cm (2½ in x 88 in) and one piece 6.5 cm x 280 cm (2½ in x 112 in) down the length of the fabric for the inner border.

STEP TWO

For each block, cut the following pieces:
- 4 of template C from the yellow fabric;
- 4 of template A from the dark scraps;
- 2 of template B from the medium scraps; and
- 2 of template B from the light scraps.

STEP THREE

Use a large flat surface to mark out the yellow fabric. Carefully trace around 240 triangles using template C, leaving space between each one for seam allowances. The cutting diagram in figure 1 will assist you with economic use of fabric. The pencil line will be your sewing line. Cut out each piece approximately 7.5 mm (¼ in) from the sewing line.

HINT

You may wish to cut all the yellow triangles first and only cut out the dark, medium and light fabrics when you are ready to piece the next block. This will eliminate storage problems for all the pieces.

PIECING
STEP ONE

Assemble the pieces for one block on a large piece of paper, using the block diagram as a guide. Use a single pin to secure each piece in place.

STEP TWO

For each block, join a C triangle to either side of an A triangle (Fig. 2). Make two of these units, using the same fabric for A each time.

STEP THREE

Join two medium and two light B triangles into a square (Fig. 3), then join an A triangle to two opposite sides, again using the same A fabric (Fig. 4).

STEP FOUR

Following the piecing diagram, join the units made in steps 2 and 3 to complete the block. Make sixty blocks.

STEP FIVE

Sew the blocks together in ten rows of six blocks each.

INNER BORDER
STEP ONE

Cut one 6.5 cm x 280 cm (2½ in x 112 in) yellow border strip in half to make two pieces 140 cm (56 in) long. Seam allowances of 7.5 mm (¼ in) are included in these measurements, as is an additional allowance of 5 cm (2 in) on either end of the strip for the mitres. Pin, then sew the borders to the top and bottom of the pieced top, matching centres and beginning and ending the stitching 7.5 mm (¼ in) from the corners. Excess fabric will extend beyond the sides of the quilt top to allow for the mitred corners. Press the borders to the right side.

STEP TWO

Attach two 220 cm (88 in) long border strips to the sides of the quilt top in a similar manner. Mitre the corners of the border. See page 151 for tips on mitring.

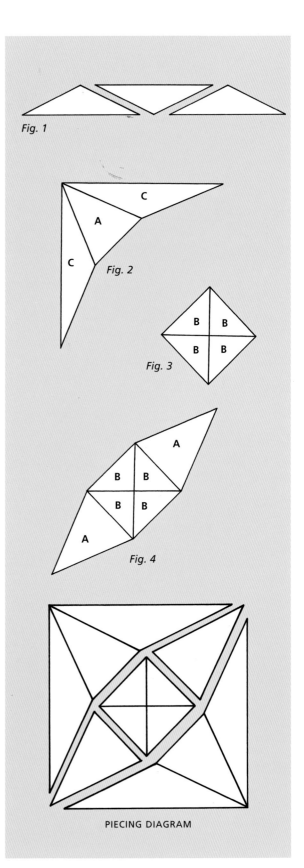

Fig. 1

Fig. 2

Fig. 3

Fig. 4

PIECING DIAGRAM

OUTER BORDER

Using the large print fabric, cut two 11.5 cm x 160 cm (4^1/$_2$ in x 64 in) and two 11.5 cm x 240 cm (4^1/$_2$ in x 96 in) strips for the outer border. Attach the outer border to the quilt top in the same way as the inner border, mitring the corners.

ASSEMBLING

STEP ONE

Cut the backing fabric into two 240 cm (96 in) lengths. Remove the selvages. Cut two 30 cm x 240 cm (12 in x 96 in) pieces from one of the lengths. Attach these two pieces on either side of the remaining 240 cm (96 in) length to make the complete backing, which is 170 cm x 240 cm (67 in x 96 in). Press.

STEP TWO

Since much of the quilting on this quilt is echo-quilting, following the outline of the piecing, 7.5 mm (^{1}/$_4$ in) wide masking tape can be used to define the quilting line. You can use the border quilting pattern photographed here or use one of your own.

Note: The centre of each block is quilted differently. Make up your own designs as you come to each block.

STEP THREE

Pin or tape the backing fabric face down on the work surface. Centre the wadding on top, then the quilt top on top of that, face upwards. Smooth out each layer as it is put down. Secure the layers of the quilt sandwich with safety pins or basting. Roll the raw edges of the quilt over onto the front and baste them in place to protect the edges during the quilting process.

QUILTING

Using the quilting thread, hoop and a quilting needle, hand-quilt the entire quilt. Begin your quilting in the centre of the quilt and work towards the edges. With most of the quilting completed, the rolled edges can be undone and the final border quilted without a hoop or a quilting frame.

TO FINISH

STEP ONE

Carefully trim the wadding and the backing to the size of the quilt top.

STEP TWO

Cut 9 cm (3^1/$_2$ in) wide binding strips and join them to create a length equal to the perimeter of the quilt, approximately 7.8 m (8^2/$_3$ yd). Fold the strip over double as you attach it to the quilt, stitching it to the right side of the quilt, and matching the raw edges. Begin attaching the binding in the centre of one side and mitre the corners. Finish by overlapping the raw edge of the binding at the beginning with 15 mm (^{1}/$_2$ in) of binding at the end. Turn under the raw edges and stitch. Turn the binding over to the quilt back, covering the stitching lines and folding tucks diagonally at the corners. Slipstitch the binding into place.

STEP THREE

Label your quilt.

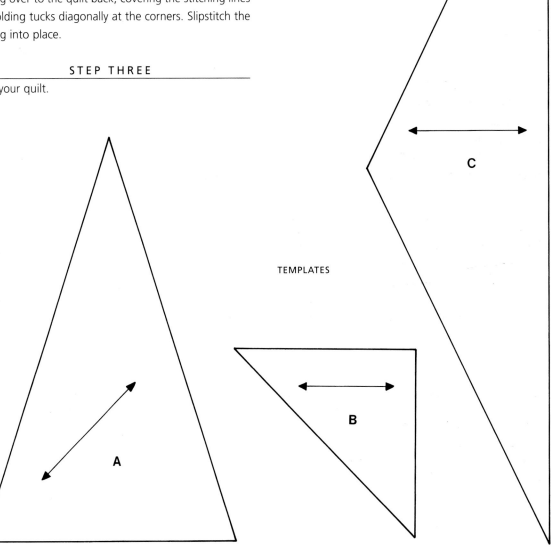

TEMPLATES

machine quilting

All the quilts in this section have been pieced on the sewing machine, many of them using the quick cutting and piecing methods which are ideally suited to quiltmaking by machine. Some of the quilts have also been machine-quilted.

The advent of the sewing machine has changed the face of quiltmaking. Not only is the sewing machine faster, it has allowed for the development of quick-piecing techniques which can see a quilt go from concept to completion in a weekend.

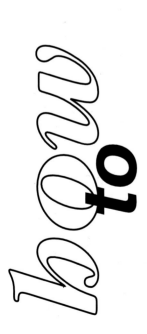

CUTTING AND PIECING

Accuracy is important and there are a few guidelines to follow to ensure success. The most important thing to establish before you begin is an accurate seam allowance.

To test if your sewing machine is sewing an accurate 7.5 mm (1/4 in) seam allowance, sew three 4 cm (1 1/2 in) wide strips of fabric together, placing the presser foot exactly on the fabric edge. Press the piece, then measure the finished width of the centre strip. It should measure exactly 2.5 cm (1 in). If not, place a marker on your sewing plate to use as a guide. Place a piece of 7.5 mm (1/4 in) graph paper under the presser foot and lower the needle into a 7.5 mm (1/4 in) marking. Stick a piece of tape exactly 7.5 mm (1/4 in) away from the needle. Remove the graph paper and use the tape as a guide for the edge of the fabric.

USING TEMPLATES

Many, if not most, machine-pieced quilts do not use templates. These are the quilts which are readily constructed from squares, rectangles, strips, and half-square or quarter-square triangles. For those quilts which have unusually shaped pieces, it is still necessary to trace and cut templates.

Trace the template given onto template plastic, using a fineline marker pen. Cut them out exactly on the marked line.

Templates for machine-piecing include a 7.5 mm (1/4 in) seam allowance. There is no marked seam line, which makes stitching an accurate 7.5 mm (1/4 in) from the cut line (edge) crucial.

QUICK CUTTING FABRIC

The quickest and most accurate way to cut fabric is with a rotary cutter, self-healing cutting mat and perspex ruler. Before you begin to cut strips for the quilt, it is essential to square up the fabric. To do this, carefully fold the fabric, selvage to selvage. Move the top layer until the fold is lying flat and the selvages are matching. You may now find that the ends of the fabric are no longer matching. Position a small square ruler as shown in figure 1, with the edge of the perspex ruler butting right up to it. Carefully remove the small ruler and using the rotary cutter, trim away the uneven ends of the fabric. You now have a perfectly square edge from which to begin cutting the pieces for your quilt.

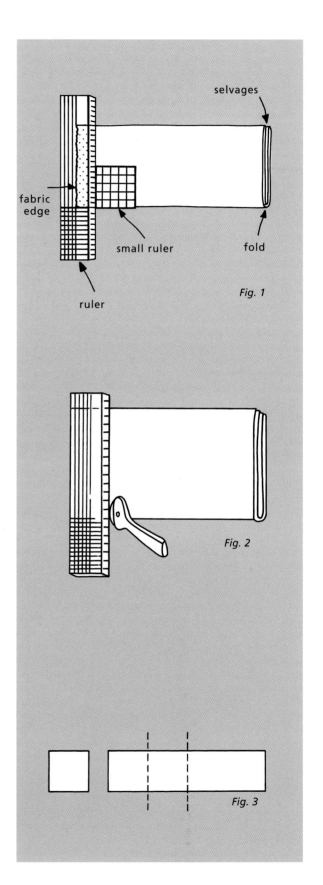

selvages

fabric edge

small ruler

fold

ruler

Fig. 1

Fig. 2

Fig. 3

CUTTING WITH A ROTARY CUTTER

Using a rotary cutter enables you to cut several thicknesses of fabric at one time. Hold the ruler in the middle and lean on it to stabilise it. Start at the folded edge of the fabric and cut away from you. The ruler must not move while you make the cut. Cut with one clean straight-through movement. Do not stop and chip away at the fabric as this will make a very untidy cut.

As the blade loses its sharpness, you will find the cutting will be harder and the blade may even develop a blunt spot where it misses cutting altogether. This is the time to invest in a new blade. If your blade is sharp and the fabric has been missed along the cut, it is because you have not put the same pressure on the blade all the way along the cutting line.

CUTTING STRIPS, SQUARES AND RECTANGLES

To cut strips, simply fold the fabric selvage to selvage, then fold it again. Place the ruler with one of the cross markings on the fold of the fabric, lining up the long 'cutting' edge at the size of the strip that you want to cut (Fig. 2).

Continue to move the ruler along the folded edge, lining the long edge up with the size strip that you want to cut. Check the straight edge occasionally to make sure that it is still straight. If you find it is no longer straight, trim it straight as before, then continue to cut all the strips that you need.

To cut squares or rectangles, cut strips of the size required for the width, then cut the strips into the required lengths. For example, to cut 5 cm (2 in) squares, cut 5 cm (2 in) wide strips, then cut them into 5 cm (2 in) squares (Fig. 3).

Remember these measurements all include seam allowances, so if you need squares with a finished size of 10 cm (4 in), cut strips 11.5 cm (4½ in) wide, then cut them into 11.5 cm (4½ in) squares.

CUTTING TRIANGLES

Many quilt designs require you to cut triangles which are joined to make squares. The easiest way to do this is to cut squares in the manner already discussed, then cut these squares into triangles. When cutting these triangles it is crucial to add the correct seam allowance plus an allowance for the points, and there are a couple of simple rules to follow.

HALF-SQUARE TRIANGLES

A square can be cut into two identical triangles whose short sides are on the straight grain and the long side on the bias. When two half-square triangles are rejoined, all four sides of the resulting square are on the straight grain. (Fig. 4).

To determine what size to cut the square for the half-square triangles, add 2.5 cm (⅞ in) to the finished measurement. For example, if you need a square with a finished size of 10 cm (4 in), cut a 12.5 cm (4⅞ in) square, then cut it in half diagonally to yield two half-square triangles.

These triangles are also often attached at the corners of a quilt with blocks set on-point to square up the quilt.

QUARTER-SQUARE TRIANGLES

A square can also be cut into four identical triangles, whose long sides are on the straight grain (Fig. 5). When four quarter-square triangles are rejoined, all four sides of the resulting square are on the straight grain.

To determine what size to cut the square for the quarter-square triangles, add 3.5 cm (1¼ in) to the finished measurement. For example, if you need a square with a finished size of 10 cm (4 in), cut a 13.5 cm (5¼ in) square, then cut it in quarters, diagonally, to yield four quarter-square triangles.

These triangles are also often attached at the sides of a quilt with blocks set on-point to square up the quilt.

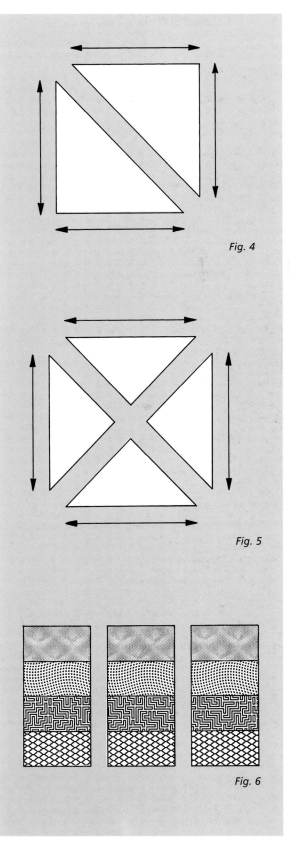

Fig. 4

Fig. 5

Fig. 6

MACHINE-PIECING

There are two easy-sewing principles you should follow:

- Sew in straight lines, avoiding sewing into corners if possible.
- Join small pieces together to form larger ones, then join those into even larger ones and continue in this way. Join patches into blocks, blocks into rows and rows into the quilt top.

Pieces are always joined with the right sides facing, except for appliqué. Backstitching is usually not necessary as seams will be crossed by other seams as more pieces are added.

STRIP-PIECING

Often, you will be sewing long strips of fabric together, then cutting them into smaller pieces.

A rotary cutter makes quick accurate cutting of multiple strips or multiple layers easy. When sewing the strips together, take care that they feed evenly through the machine, otherwise you may produce a banana-shaped fabric. A walking foot on your sewing machine may help to feed the layers of fabric through evenly.

Sew with an accurate seam allowance and press all the seam allowances in the same direction.

To cut lengths from the strip-pieced fabric, use the ruler and rotary cutter and treat the pieced fabric as if it were a single piece (Fig. 6)

CHAIN-PIECING

You can save time and thread by chain-piecing patches together. Place the pieces that are to be joined with right sides together and sew across one strip. Do not lift the presser foot or cut the threads, just feed in the next two pieces as close as possible to the last pair. Sew as many of these as you can before you cut the thread (Fig. 7).

MATCHING SEAM LINES

Inevitably, you will have to sew across seam lines when you are piecing a quilt. When you come to such a point, push one seam allowance to one side, usually towards the darker side, and the other seam allowance the other way, matching the seam lines. A little bit of pull or push to match these seams will make sure that you have all the cross seams meeting (Fig. 8).

PRESSING

Always press as you go to keep the pieces flat and the seams as sharp as possible. Press the seams to one side, usually towards the darker fabric. When the pieces are cut on the bias, be particularly careful with your pressing as these pieces can easily be pressed out of shape.

BORDERS

Specific instructions are given for the borders of each quilt. Though approximate lengths are given for borders, always measure your quilt top through the centre to get the exact measurement. For more information about borders, see page 151.

QUILTING

Machine-quilting is often used simply to hold all the layers together, but some quilters create fabulous effects with machine-quilting. Machine-quilting is generally of two types: straight-line and free machine.

Straight-line quilting is worked around the blocks and borders, in-the-ditch, or in parallel lines to form a grid. A walking foot is helpful with machine-quilting, if you are stitching in a straight line. Keep the feed dogs up and stitch through all layers of the quilt.

Free machine-quilting is used to create intricate patterns or all-over effects, such as stippling. Drop the feed dogs on the sewing machine and use a darning foot. Do not turn the fabric to follow the design, but guide the quilt with your hands, imitating the tension created by a hoop. Practise this technique first on a piece of fabric with wadding behind it. You will have to move the fabric through the machine, so practise going forward and backwards, then from side to side. Try to keep the length of the stitches even. Once you have mastered control of the machine with the feed dogs lowered, this is a quicker way of quilting, as you are not turning the large quilt through the machine all the time.

Make sure you machine-quilt in the same direction across the quilt to minimise shifting of the layers.

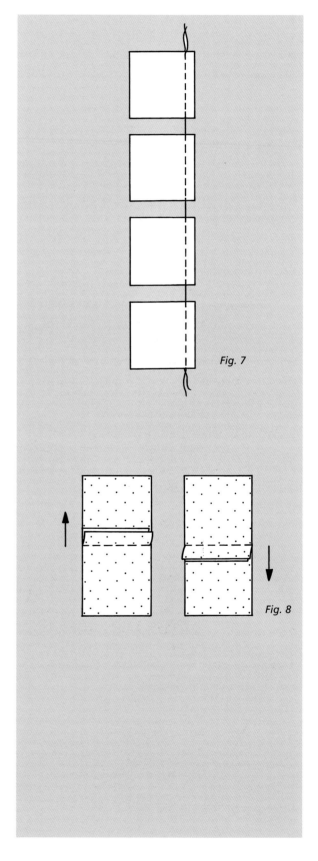

Fig. 7

Fig. 8

PREPARING FOR QUILTING

Press the quilt top when you have sewn the borders on. This will be your last opportunity to get it good and flat.

There is no need to mark the quilt top if you are quilting in-the-ditch or quilting around shapes and blocks. For quilting a grid, most quilters use 7.5 mm (1/4 in) masking tape to mark the lines.

Some fabrics are difficult to mark because they are so busy. If you want to quilt a design on such a fabric, you can cut out the quilting design from tissue paper and pin it directly onto the quilt. Quilt around it, then when the quilting is completed, tear the tissue paper away.

When the marking is completed, assemble and secure the quilt sandwich (see page 151).

Make sure your sewing machine is in good working order. Clean the bobbin area of fluff and thread and insert a new needle.

Set up your sewing area properly. With the exception of some very small quilts, most quilts will require you to manipulate considerable bulk under the machine. Having a work area which provides support for the quilt will help considerably.

These days, it is possible to buy a monofilament thread (invisible thread) from quilt shops. Do not use the one that is sold on the small cotton reels for mending – it is too thick. Invisible thread has the obvious advantage of not being seen so, if you go off the line slightly, it will not show up. It will also save you a lot of time and trouble as it will go through all colours of fabric. If you cannot buy the invisible thread, use a thread to match the quilt top.

You may need to adjust the length of your stitch and, if you are using the monofilament thread, you may need to loosen the top tension a little. If the bobbin thread is pulling up to the top, put the top tension down just one number. For Bernina machines, thread the bobbin thread through the hole in the arm of the bobbin case as you do for buttonholes.

GETTING STARTED

It is best to plan your stitching so that you are always working in the one direction and, as far as possible, the bulk of the quilt is always on the left side.

Begin by stitching right around the quilt 7.5 mm (1/4 in) from the edge. This will hold all the layers securely together while you work. If possible, divide the quilt into halves or quarters with lines of quilting, so you have an area in which to work.

Roll up the sides of the quilt tightly on either side of the presser foot and begin quilting in the centre of the quilt. Hold the quilt taut and flat as you work, and regularly check that you have not made any puckers on the back. Work on one area at a time rolling and unrolling the quilt, and removing the safety pins, as required.

To start and stop a line of quilting, you can either stitch a few tiny stitches on one spot or leave tails of thread, which you can later pull to the back and tie off.

Stitch slowly and stop frequently to readjust the quilt.

When all the quilting is completed, remove the last of the safety pins.

TYING

Some quilts are not quilted at all in the traditional sense, but they are tied. This is particularly useful for quilts where a very thick wadding has been used. Using heavy crochet cotton, take a stitch through all the layers of the quilt, then tie the ends together securely twice. Don't pull too tightly. Trim the ends. For very dramatic tufts, use several strands of thread or very thick thread. You can tie a quilt using matching or contrasting cotton. Tie in the seam line or in the centre of the patch, depending on whether you are making a feature of the tying or not. You can tie your quilt on the top, for a feature, or on the back, if you do not want the tufts to show.

GRID QUILTING

FREE MACHINE-QUILTING

9-patch scrap quilt

BY KATE McEWEN

This quilt has been Kate's 'take along' project for more than three years. 'I have become addicted to buying those packs of five-inch squares of fabric from quilt shops,' she says.

The four smaller patches in the block can be cut from one of these squares, but the five larger patches must be cut out of a larger piece.

Even though this is a scrap quilt, it is still better to work with good cotton fabrics, not just any old dress fabrics which may cause problems with fraying and ironing. It is also better to stick to the same weight of fabric throughout.

This quilt is machine-pieced and machine-quilted.

FINISHED SIZE

Quilt: 210 cm x 275 cm (84 in x 110 in)
Block size: 15 cm (6 in) square
Total number of pieced blocks: eighty-eight

FABRIC REQUIREMENTS

13 cm (5 in) squares of cotton fabrics or scraps large enough to cut into four 6.5 cm (2^1/$_2$ in) squares
Scraps large enough to cut into five 6.5 cm (2^1/$_2$ in) squares
2.5 m (2^3/$_4$ yd) of cream print fabric
3 m (3^1/$_4$ yd) each of a cream print fabric and a multi-coloured print fabric for the borders
5.6 m (6^1/$_4$ yd) of fabric for the backing
110 cm (44 in) of fabric for the binding
245 cm x 310 cm (97 in x 122 in) of wadding

OTHER REQUIREMENTS

Quilter's ruler
Pencil
Rotary cutter
Self-healing cutting mat
Scissors
Matching sewing thread
Quilting thread
4 cm (1^1/$_2$ in) safety pins
Glass-headed pins
Masking tape

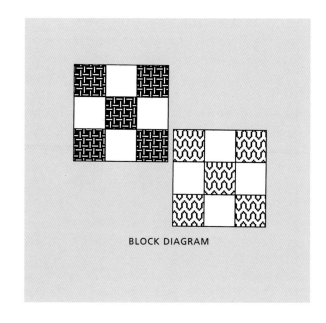

BLOCK DIAGRAM

CUTTING

Note: 7.5 mm (^{1}/$_4$ in) seam allowances are included in the measurements.

STEP ONE

For each block, cut a 13 cm (5 in) square into four squares and one of the scrap fabrics into five 6.5 cm (2^1/$_2$ in) squares. Alternatively, from one scrap fabric, cut four 6.5 cm (2^1/$_2$ in) squares and, from another scrap fabric, cut five 6.5 cm (2^1/$_2$ in) squares.

STEP TWO

From the cream fabric, cut the following pieces:
• twelve 16.5 cm (6^1/$_2$ in) wide strips across the width of the fabric, cut into seventy 16.5 cm (6^1/$_2$ in) squares;
• three 24 cm (9^1/$_2$ in) wide strips across the width of the fabric, cut into nine 24 cm (9^1/$_2$ in) squares, cut into quarters along both diagonals to yield quarter-square triangles for the side triangles (Fig. 1); and
• two 11 cm (5^1/$_8$ in) squares, cut in half, diagonally, to yield four half-square triangles for the corners.

PIECING

STEP ONE

Sew the pieced 16.5 cm (6¹/₂ in) 9-patch blocks. Make eighty-eight of these pieced blocks.

STEP TWO

Sew the blocks together into diagonal rows, alternating 9-patch blocks with plain blocks and placing a quarter-square triangle at each end of each row (Fig. 2). Continue adding rows of blocks to the quilt until there are eleven rows down, then start to square off the quilt.

STEP THREE

Join the half-square corner triangles to the corners of the quilt to complete the quilt top.

BORDERS

STEP ONE

Measure the length of the quilt top, measuring through the centre. Cut the inner side borders 6.5 cm (2¹/₂ in) wide by this length, down the length of the fabric. Attach the side borders. Measure, cut and sew the top and bottom borders in the same way as the side borders.

STEP TWO

Measure, cut and sew the 16.5 cm (6¹/₂ in) wide outer borders as for the inner borders. Press the quilt top carefully to avoid stretching it.

ASSEMBLING

STEP ONE

Cut the backing fabric into two pieces, lengthwise, then rejoin the pieces, sewing the selvages together. Press the seam flat. The join will go down the quilt back.

STEP TWO

Pin or tape the backing face down on the work surface. Centre the wadding on top. You may have to join wadding pieces to achieve the total width. If you do, butt the two edges together and use herringbone stitch to join them. Do not overlap the edges. If the wadding is not too thick, it can sometimes be zigzagged together on your sewing machine.

STEP THREE

Place the quilt top on the other layers, face upwards. Smooth out all the layers as you place them. Secure the layers of the quilt sandwich, using the safety pins.

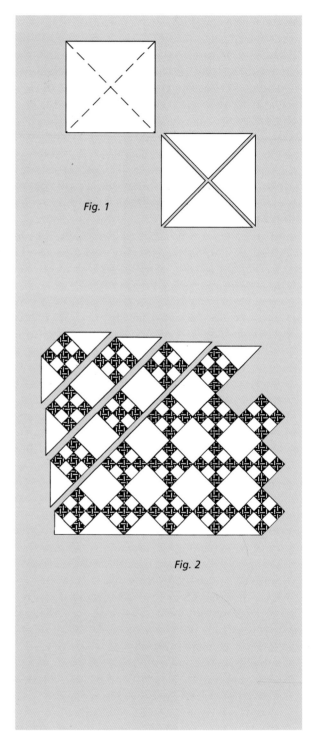

Fig. 1

Fig. 2

QUILTING

Machine-quilt in straight lines going along the small squares and straight across the plain squares. Machine-quilting with a large quilt, such as this one, is not always easy. Work from the centre of the quilt to the sides, rolling the sides of the quilt into a tight roll to get to the centre. Using a thin wadding will also help.

HINT

9-patch blocks can also be made very simply using the strip-piecing method. Cut 6.5 cm (2¹/2 in) wide strips across the width of the fabrics. Join them, lengthwise, alternating the fabrics as shown in figure 3. Cross-cut the strips into 6.5 cm (2¹/2 in) wide units (Fig. 4). Rejoin the units to make up the 9-patch block (Fig. 5).

TO FINISH
STEP ONE

Trim the wadding and the backing to the size of the quilt top. Measure the width and length of the quilt top and cut 9 cm (3¹/2 in) wide strips for the binding to these lengths. You will need to join strips to achieve the correct length of binding required.

STEP TWO

Press the binding strips over double with the wrong sides together. Sew the binding to the edges of the right side of the quilt with the raw edges even and being extremely careful not to stretch the quilt edges. Sew the binding on all four sides, then turn the folded edge of the binding to the back of the quilt. Slipstitch the binding in place, mitring the corners.

STEP THREE

Label your quilt.

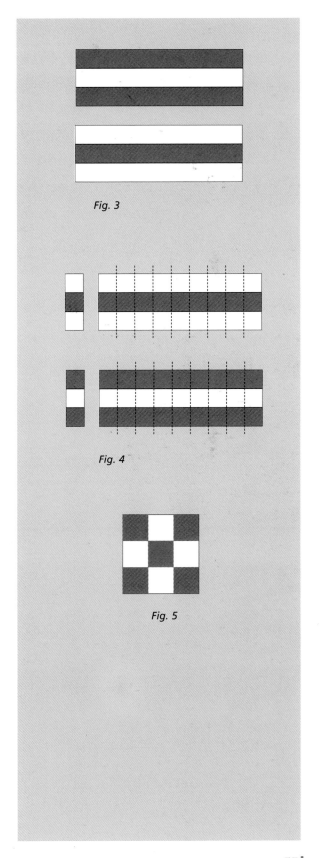

Fig. 3

Fig. 4

Fig. 5

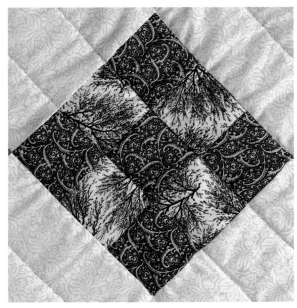

THE PIECED 9-PATCH BLOCK

english ivy

BY KATE McEWEN

This is a very graceful and charming quilt design, with its stylised lilies. The peach-coloured, plain squares in this quilt are the perfect places to show off beautiful quilting and the two greens add contrast on the otherwise plain quilt.

You can create quite a different effect, making the design in bright colours.

This quilt is machine-pieced and hand-quilted.

FINISHED SIZE

Quilt: 170 cm x 218 cm (68 in x 86 in)

Block size: 30 cm (12 in) square

Total number of blocks: twelve

FABRIC REQUIREMENTS

60 cm (24 in) of dark green fabric

60 cm (24 in) of light green fabric

110 cm (44 in) of off-white fabric for the background

236 cm (93 in) of peach fabric for the plain blocks, triangles and inner border

220 cm (87 in) of fabric for the outer border

4.5 m (5 yd) of fabric for the backing

60 cm (24 in) of fabric for the binding

179 cm x 226 cm (70 in x 89 in) of wadding

OTHER REQUIREMENTS

Quilter's ruler

Pencil or water-soluble marker pen

Rotary cutter

Self-healing cutting mat

Scissors

Matching sewing thread

Hand-quilting thread

Quilting needles

Quilting hoop

4 cm (1½ in) safety pins

Glass-headed pins

Stencil for hand-quilting (optional)

Masking tape

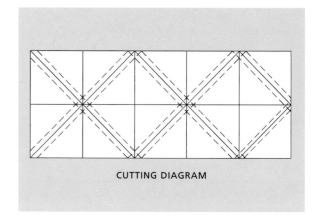

CUTTING DIAGRAM

CUTTING

STEP ONE

You will need 108 squares that are made up of a dark green triangle and an off-white triangle for the ivy tips. To form these squares, cut 40 cm (16 in) off the end of the dark green fabric and set the rest aside for the stalks. Cut a 40 cm (16 in) width across the off-white fabric as well.

STEP TWO

Pin the 40 cm (16 in) widths of the dark green and the off-white fabric together with the right sides facing. Using the pencil and ruler, draw the diagram in the cutting diagram on to the wrong side of the off-white fabric along the 40 cm (16 in) length but 2.5 cm (1 in) above the selvage. Draw ten 7.5 cm (2⅞ in) squares as shown in the diagram. Draw in the solid diagonal lines. Draw in the dotted lines 7.5 mm (¼ in) on either side of the solid lines – these are your sewing lines.

STEP THREE

Stitch along one dotted line, beginning at the bottom left-hand corner of the diagram, stitching all the way up, then down all the way, then up to the halfway point, then work your way back to the upper left-hand corner in one continuous line of stitching. Jump over the solid line and stitch along the other dotted line.

STEP FOUR

Cut the ten squares apart along the vertical and horizontal solid lines, then cut them in half along the diagonal solid lines. Lay each square on the ironing board

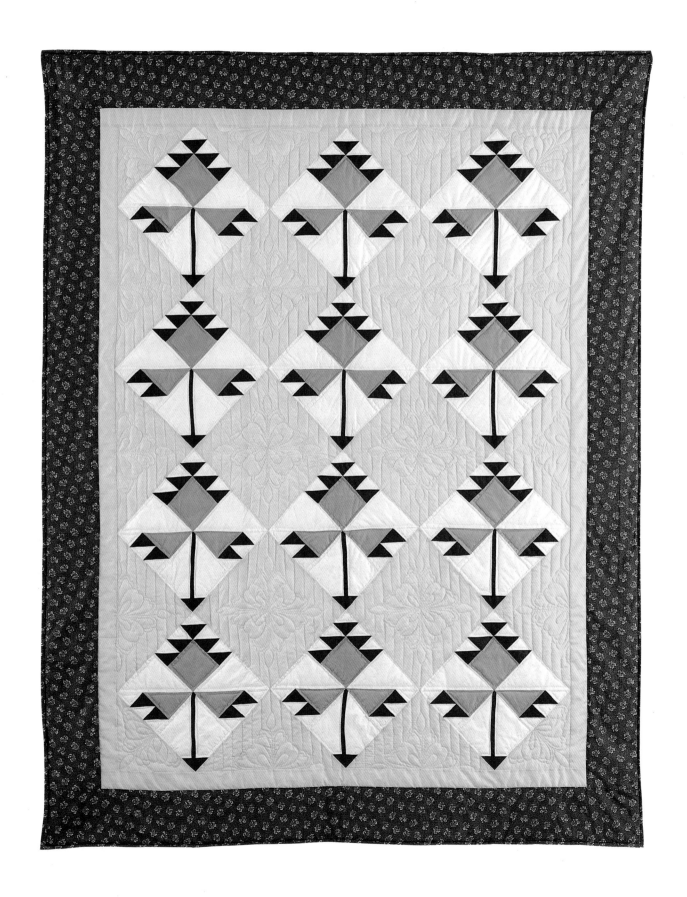

english ivy

with the darker side uppermost. Pick up the dark corner and run the iron across the square. This way you will always press the seam allowance towards the darker side. Make 108 of these squares.

STEP FIVE

From the off-white fabric, cut the following pieces:
- one 7.5 cm (2^7/$_8$ in) strip across the width of the fabric, cut into 7.5 cm (2^7/$_8$ in) squares, cut in half, diagonally, to yield twenty-four half-square triangles;
- twelve 16.5 cm (6^1/$_2$ in) squares; and
- twelve 17.5 cm (6^7/$_8$ in) squares, cut in half, diagonally, to yield twenty-four half-square triangles.

STEP SIX

From the light green fabric, cut the following pieces:
- twelve 11.5 cm (4^1/$_2$ in) squares; and
- twelve 12.5 cm (4^7/$_8$ in) squares, cut in half, diagonally, to yield twenty-four half-square triangles.

STEP SEVEN

From the dark green fabric you had set aside for the stems, cut the following pieces:
- twelve 4 cm (1^1/$_2$ in) wide bias strips; and
- twelve 6.5 cm (2^1/$_2$ in) squares for the base triangles.

STEP EIGHT

From the peach fabric, cut the following pieces:
- four 6.5 cm (2^1/$_2$ in) wide strips along the length of the fabric for the inner border;
- six 31.5 cm (12^1/$_2$ in) squares;
- three 47 cm (18^1/$_2$ in) squares, cut into quarters along both diagonals, to yield twelve side triangles; and
- two 24 cm (9^1/$_2$ in) squares, cut in half, diagonally, to yield four corner triangles.

PIECING

STEP ONE

Join two small dark green and white squares (Fig. 1) and three small dark green and white squares together (Fig. 2). Join these to two adjoining sides of a light green square (Fig. 3).

STEP TWO

Join a small off-white triangle on one end of two small dark green and white squares (Fig. 4), then join the strip to one side of a light green triangle (Fig. 5). Join a large off-white triangle to the long side of this piece to form a square (Fig. 6). Make two of these squares, noting that they are mirror images of one another.

STEP THREE

Turn under and press a 7.5 mm (1/4 in) seam allowance on both sides of the bias strip for the stem. Hand-appliqué the stem along the diagonal of the large off-white square. Place one dark green base square in the lower right-hand corner of the cream square over the end of the stem. Stitch across the base square from corner to corner, on the opposite diagonal to the stem. Press the upper half triangle of the base square over the lower half triangle, even with the sides of the square. Cut out the lower half green triangle to reduce bulk.

STEP FOUR

Following the piecing diagram, join the four squares you made in steps 1, 2 and 3 to form the complete block. Make twelve blocks the same.

STEP FIVE

Piece the quilt top, following the photograph, making diagonal rows of alternating pieced and plain blocks. Add the peach side triangles at the ends of the rows and the peach half-square triangles at the corners to complete the quilt top. Press well.

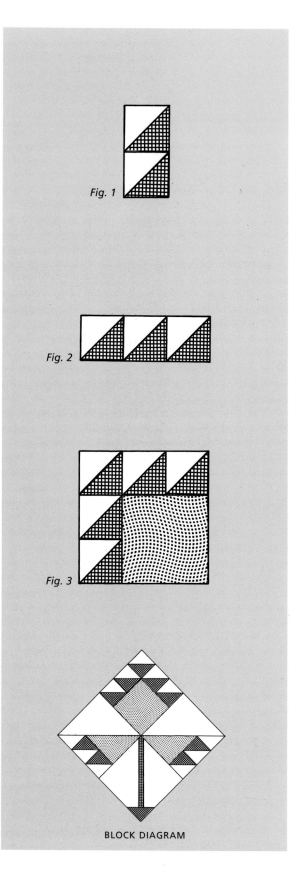

Fig. 1

Fig. 2

Fig. 3

BLOCK DIAGRAM

BORDERS

STEP ONE

Measure the length of the quilt top, measuring through the centre. Cut 6.5 cm (2½ in) wide peach side borders to this length, then sew them on. Measure the width of the quilt top, measuring through the centre, then cut the top and bottom peach borders to this width. Sew on the top and bottom borders.

STEP TWO

Measure, cut and sew the 16.5 cm (6½ in) wide outer border in the same way as the inner border. Press the finished quilt top.

QUILTING

See the quilting design on Pull Out Pattern Sheet 1.

STEP ONE

Using the pencil or fabric marker pen, lightly trace the quilting pattern onto the plain squares, before you assemble the layers of the quilt.

STEP TWO

Cut the length of the backing fabric in half, then rejoin it to double the width. Press the seam open. Pin or tape the backing face down on the work surface. Centre the wadding on top and the quilt on top of that, facing upwards. Smooth out each layer as you place it. Pin the three layers together, using the safety pins.

STEP THREE

Begin the hand-quilting in the centre of the quilt, using a quilting hoop. Move the hoop to the next square as you finish each one. The off-white triangles in the quilt have been hand-quilted around the outline of the triangle.

TO FINISH

STEP ONE

When the quilting is completed, trim the backing and the wadding to the size of the quilt top.

STEP TWO

Cut 9 cm (3½ in) wide strips for the binding, measuring the length as before. Fold the binding strip over double with the wrong sides together and the raw edges even. Sew the binding to the right side of the quilt with raw edges even. Sew on all four sides, then turn the folded edge of the binding to the back of the quilt and slipstitch it in place.

STEP THREE

Label your quilt.

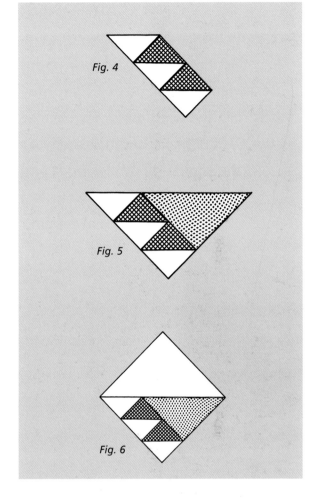

Fig. 4

Fig. 5

Fig. 6

THE PIECED BLOCK

THE QUILTING DESIGN

BY KATE McEWEN

Everyone likes a blue and white quilt, but this one is a little different because it actually uses a light grey fabric for the background. Kate chose the Gemini block because she liked the challenge of piecing it and because one of her sons is a real Gemini!

This quilt uses three different blue fabrics plus a light grey for the background. It works well with the hint of shadow in the blocks.

This quilt is machine-pieced and machine-quilted.

FINISHED SIZE

Quilt: 145 cm x 195 cm (58 in x 78 in)
Block size: 25 cm (10 in) square
Total number of blocks: twenty-four

FABRIC REQUIREMENTS

90 cm (36 in) of mid-blue fabric for the kite shapes
90 cm (36 in) of bright blue fabric for the kite shapes
2.2 m (2 1/2 yd) of dark blue fabric for the centre squares, the outer border and the binding
2 m (2 1/4 yd) of light grey fabric for the background and inner border
3 m (3 1/2 yd) of fabric for the backing
150 cm x 200 cm (1 2/3 yd x 2 1/4 yd) of wadding

OTHER REQUIREMENTS

Quilter's ruler
Rotary cutter
Self-healing cutting mat
Fineline permanent marker pen
Pencil or water-soluble marker pen
Template plastic
Scissors
Matching sewing thread
Quilting thread
4 cm (1 1/2 in) safety pins
Glass-headed pins
Masking tape

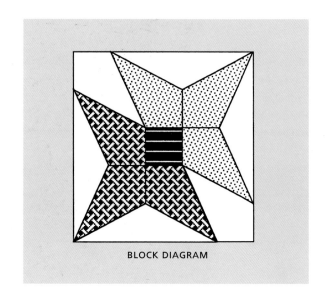

BLOCK DIAGRAM

MAKING TEMPLATES

See the templates on page 63. Add 7.5 mm (1/4 in) seam allowances when you cut them from fabric.

Trace the templates A, B and C onto the template plastic, using the permanent marker pen. Carefully cut them out along the marked line.

CUTTING

STEP ONE

Using template A, cut seventy-two kite shapes from each of the bright blue and mid-blue fabrics.

STEP TWO

From the light grey fabric, cut the following pieces:
- four 9 cm (3 1/2 in) wide strips for the inner border;
- 48 of template A; and
- 96 of template B.

STEP THREE

From the dark blue fabric, cut the following pieces:
- four 16.5 cm (6 1/2 in) wide strips by the length of the fabric for the outer borders; and
- 24 of template C.

gemini blue

gemini blue

PIECING

Note: Take care with the set-in seams in this block. To help you, you can mark with a pencil or the water-soluble pen the 7.5 mm ($\frac{1}{4}$ in) seam point at the corners which have to be set in.

STEP ONE

Join two mid-blue A pieces together as shown (Fig. 1). Join on a light grey A piece (Fig. 2). Join on a light grey B piece (Fig. 3).

STEP TWO

Join another mid-blue A piece and a light grey B piece to the set made in step 1 (Fig. 4). Make another set the same, using the bright blue fabric.

STEP THREE

Join both sets together with a square C piece to form the complete block.

STEP FOUR

Make twenty-four of these blocks. Sew the blocks together in six rows of four blocks each, carefully matching the points. A correct seam allowance is very important in this quilt.

BORDERS

STEP ONE

Measure the length of the quilt top, measuring through the centre. Cut the light grey border strips to this length. Stitch them to the sides of the quilt top. Measure, cut and sew the top and bottom borders in the same way as for the side borders.

STEP TWO

Measure, cut and sew the dark blue outer borders in the same way. Press the quilt top very gently to avoid stretching the edges.

ASSEMBLING

STEP ONE

Cut the backing fabric in half, lengthwise, then rejoin the pieces to double the width. Press the seam open.

STEP TWO

Pin or tape the backing, face down, on the work surface. Centre the wadding on top. Place the quilt top on top, facing upwards. Smooth out all the layers as you put them down. Secure the layers of the quilt sandwich, using the safety pins.

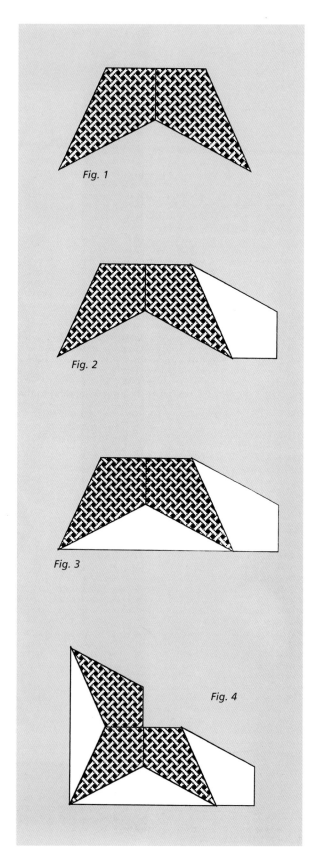

Fig. 1

Fig. 2

Fig. 3

Fig. 4

THE PIECED BLOCK

QUILTING

Begin machine-quilting in the centre of the quilt. Roll up the sides of the quilt tightly to allow you to reach into the centre. Quilt around the shapes, stitching 'in-the-ditch'. This will make the stars stand out. Quilting around the seam line between the borders will also help keep the quilt together.

TO FINISH

STEP ONE

Trim the wadding and the quilt backing to the size of the quilt top.

STEP TWO

Measure for the binding in the same way as for the borders. Cut 9 cm (3^{1}/2 in) wide strips from the remaining dark blue fabric. Join the binding strips to achieve the desired length. Fold the strips over double with the wrong sides together and raw edges even. Sew the bindings to the right side of the quilt sides, with the raw edges together. Stitch all four sides, then turn the binding to the back of the quilt. Slipstitch it in place, mitring the corners.

STEP THREE

Label your quilt.

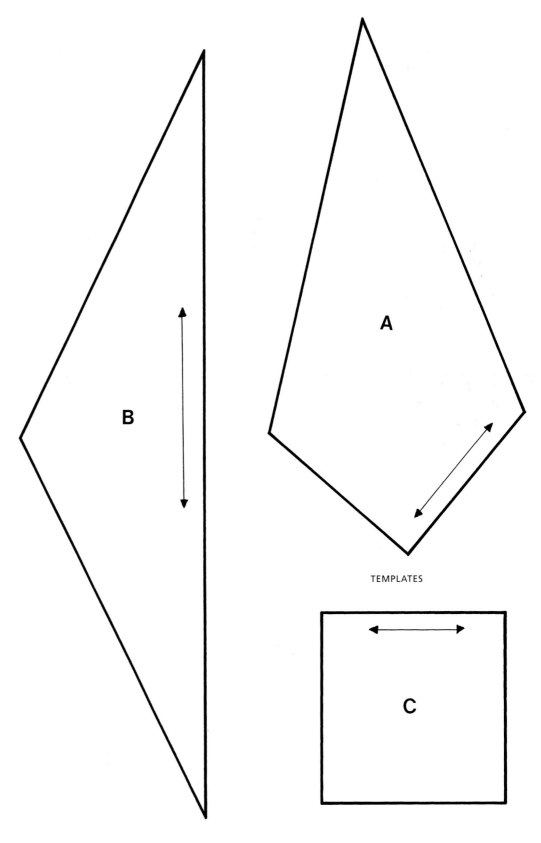

TEMPLATES

BY KATE McEWEN

The bargello design in this quilted wallhanging comes from a traditional needlework pattern which is usually worked on canvas with wool. You can design some very interesting effects, using this method.

in the red

Be imaginative when choosing fabric for this quilt, but there are some pitfalls to be aware of. Kate used a small piece of silver lamé to add interest to the red and black, but lamé is very hard to work with. It frays badly and shrivels up if it comes in contact with heat, such as the iron. This makes pressing very difficult. Ironing a lightweight interfacing onto the back of the lamé, before cutting out any strips will make it much easier to handle.

FINISHED SIZE

Quilt: 140 cm x 196 cm (55 in x 77 in)
This quilt is machine-pieced and machine-quilted.

FABRIC REQUIREMENTS

40 cm (16 in) each of thirteen different fabrics, ranging in colour from black to light grey and two different red fabrics
20 cm (8 in) of silver lamé or a similar highlight fabric
2 m (2^1/4 yd) of light grey fabric for the inner border
2 m (2^1/4 yd) of black fabric for the outer border
3 m (3^1/4 yd) of fabric for the backing
70 cm (28 in) of fabric for the binding
150 cm x 210 cm (59 in x 83 in) of wadding

OTHER REQUIREMENTS

Quilter's ruler
Pencil or water-soluble marker pen
Rotary cutter
Self-healing cutting mat
Scissors
Matching sewing thread
Monofilament thread for quilting
Pressing cloth
Usual sewing supplies
Masking tape
4 cm (1^1/2 in) safety pins

CUTTING
STEP ONE

First arrange the colours in the order that you are going to use them. Cut off a tiny sample of each one and stick them on a sheet of paper in the same order, to use as a guide. Kate used an arrangement of colours that goes from dark to light, then dark to light again.

STEP TWO

Using the rotary cutter and self-healing mat, cut eight 5 cm (2 in) wide strips across the full width of the fabric from each of the fabrics, except the lamé, from which you should cut four strips. Join the strips into four sets in the same order that you have determined. Each fabric appears twice in each set, except the lamé which only appears once. Press each set well with all the seams going in the same direction. Take great care when pressing the lamé – use a pressing cloth.

STEP THREE

Using the rotary cutter and self-healing mat, cut the following strips from the pieced sets:
- three 10 cm (4 in) wide;
- six 7.5 cm (3 in) wide;
- six 6.5 cm (2^1/2 in) wide;
- six 5 cm (2 in) wide;
- six 4.5 cm (1^3/4 in) wide;
- six 4 cm (1^1/2 in) wide;
- six 2.5 cm (1 in) wide; and
- three 2 cm (^{3}/4 in) wide.
  Set all these pieces aside.

PIECING
STEP ONE

Put aside one of the 10 cm (4 in) strips with the darkest colour at the bottom. Join the narrower edges of all the other strips to form circles (Fig. 1).

STEP TWO

Take the first 10 cm (4 in) piece that you set aside and is not sewn into a circle and the first 7.5 cm (3 in) wide circle. Find the starting point of the first strip on the circle and undo the next seam up. Join these two strips together. Continue joining the next size circle/strip to the last one, undoing the next seam up every time. This makes the colours move up and down the quilt (Fig. 2).

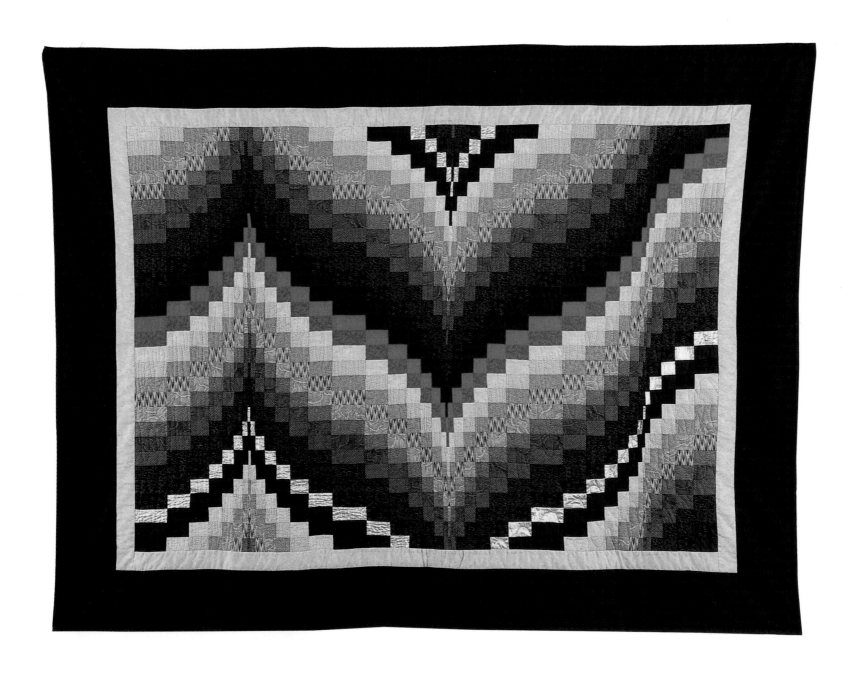

Join the pieces in the following order:

In centimetres

10 cm to 7.5 cm to 6.5 cm to 5 cm to 4.5 cm to 4 cm to 2.5 cm to 2 cm to 2.5 cm to 4 cm to 4.5 cm to 5 cm to 6.5 cm to 7.5 cm to 10 cm to 7.5 cm to 6.5 cm to 5 cm to 4.5 cm to 4 cm to 2.5 cm to 2 cm to 2.5 cm to 4 cm to 4.5 cm to 5 cm to 6.5 cm to 7.5 cm to 10 cm to 7.5 cm to 6.5 cm to 5 cm to 4.5 cm to 4 cm to 2.5 cm to 2 cm to 2.5 cm to 4 cm to 4.5 cm to 5 cm to 6.5 cm to 7.5 cm

In inches

4 in to 3 in to 2$\frac{1}{2}$ in to 2 in to 1$\frac{3}{4}$ in to 1$\frac{1}{2}$ in to 1 in to $\frac{3}{4}$ in to 1 in to 1$\frac{1}{2}$ in to 1$\frac{3}{4}$ in to 2 in to 2$\frac{1}{2}$ in to 3 in to 4 in to 3 in to 2$\frac{1}{2}$ in to 2 in to 1$\frac{3}{4}$ in to 1$\frac{1}{2}$ in to 1 in to $\frac{3}{4}$ in to 1 in to 1$\frac{1}{2}$ in to 1$\frac{3}{4}$ in to 2 in to 2$\frac{1}{2}$ in to 3 in to 4 in to 3 in to 2$\frac{1}{2}$ in to 2 in to 1$\frac{3}{4}$ in to 1$\frac{1}{2}$ in to 1 in to $\frac{3}{4}$ in to 1 in to 1$\frac{1}{2}$ in to 1$\frac{3}{4}$ in to 2 in to 2$\frac{1}{2}$ in to 3 in.

STEP THREE

When all the pieces are joined together, press the quilt top well but remember to take care with the lamé.

BORDERS

STEP ONE

Measure the width of the quilt top, measuring through the centre. Cut the 6.5 cm (2$\frac{1}{2}$ in) wide inner borders to this length, then join them to the top and bottom of the quilt. Measure, cut and sew the side borders in the same way as for the top and bottom borders.

STEP TWO

Measure and cut the 16.5 cm (6$\frac{1}{2}$ in) wide outer borders and join them to the top and bottom of the quilt top. Measure, cut and sew the side borders in the same way as for the top and bottom borders. Press carefully again.

ASSEMBLING

Cut the backing fabric in half, lengthwise, then rejoin the pieces to double the width. Press the seam allowance flat. Pin or tape the backing face down on the work surface. Centre the wadding on top. Place the quilt top on top of that, facing upwards. Smooth out each layer as you put it down. Secure the layers of the quilt sandwich with the safety pins.

QUILTING

Drop the feed dogs on your sewing machine and put on the darning foot. Using either matching thread or the monofilament thread, free machine-stitch across the surface of the quilt.

TO FINISH

STEP ONE

Trim the backing and wadding to the size of the quilt top. Measure and cut the 9 cm (3$\frac{1}{2}$ in) wide binding in the same way as for the borders. Fold the binding over double with the wrong sides together and the raw edges even. Sew the binding to all four edges of the right sides of the quilt with raw edges even, then turn the folded edge of the binding to the back of the quilt and slipstitch it in place, mitring the corners.

STEP TWO

If you want to hang the quilt, sew a sleeve on the back of the quilt to pass a rod through. See how to make a hanging sleeve on page 153.

STEP THREE

Label your quilt.

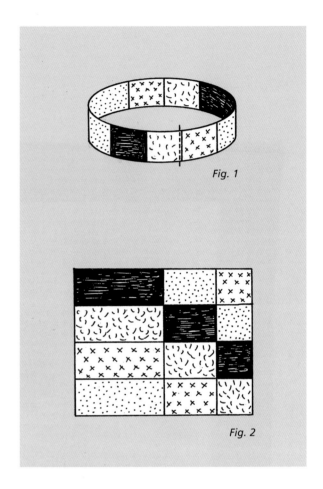

Fig. 1

Fig. 2

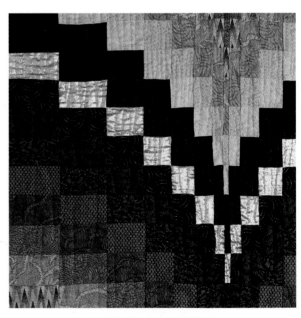

CLOSE-UP OF THE PIECING

BY LYNNE PEEBLES

The block used in this wonderful quilt is a variation of the traditional Lady of the Lake pattern. It is an ideal quilt to make from scrap fabrics.

which way did they go?

Use as many different fabrics as you can. Lynne has used strong jewel-like colours to contrast with the black triangles and borders.

This quilt is machine-pieced and machine-quilted.

FINISHED SIZE

Quilt: 158 cm x 238 cm (60 in x 90 in)
Block size: 40 cm (15 in) square
Total number of blocks: fifteen

FABRIC REQUIREMENTS

Scraps of six fabrics of the same colour tones, ranging from light to dark, for each block
2.5 m (2²/3 yd) of fabric for the borders
5 m (5¹/2 yd) of fabric for the backing
80 cm (32 in) of fabric for the binding
168 cm x 248 cm (64 in x 94 in) of wadding

OTHER REQUIREMENTS

Quilter's ruler
Pencil or water-soluble marker pen
Rotary cutter
Self-healing cutting mat
Scissors
Matching sewing thread
Quilting thread
4 cm (1¹/2 in) safety pins
Glass-headed pins
Masking tape

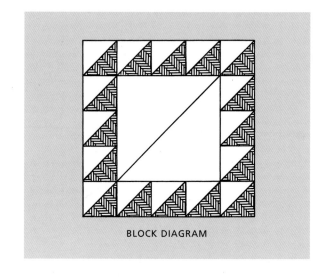

BLOCK DIAGRAM

CUTTING

Note: 7.5 mm (¹/4 in) seam allowances are included in the measurements.

STEP ONE

Choose two colours for each block. Arrange the scrap fabrics in those colours ranging from the lightest (1) through to the darkest (6). For example, you should have six shades of red and six shades of blue.

STEP TWO

Place 1 and 6 together with the right sides facing. Using the quilter's ruler, mark a 14.5 cm (5³/8 in) square on both fabrics, then cut them out. Mark the diagonal, then stitch 7.5 mm (¹/4 in) on either side of the marked diagonal. Cut along the diagonal line and open out the two squares. Press the seam allowance over onto the darker of the two fabrics. The squares with small half-square triangles will form the centre of two Lady of the Lake blocks. Make sixty of these squares in the other scrap fabrics.

STEP THREE

Group fabrics 2, 3, 4, and 5 into light and dark pairs. Pin each pair of fabrics together with the right sides facing. Using the pencil or water-soluble marker pen and ruler, draw the diagram in figure 1 onto the wrong side of the lighter fabric. Draw ten 6.5 cm (2³/8 in) squares as shown in the diagram. Draw in the solid diagonal lines and the dotted lines 7.5 mm (¹/4 in) on either side of the solid lines – these are your sewing lines.

which way did they go?

STEP FOUR

Stitch along one dotted line, beginning at the bottom left-hand corner of the diagram, stitching all the way up, then down all the way, then up to the halfway point, then work your way back to the upper left-hand corner in one continuous line of stitching. Jump over the solid line and stitch along the other dotted line.

STEP FIVE

Cut the ten squares apart along the vertical and horizontal solid lines, then cut them in half along the diagonal solid lines. Lay each square on the ironing board with the darker side uppermost. Pick up the dark corner and run the iron across the square. This way you will always press the seam allowance towards the darker side. Make eight squares of half-square triangles from each pair. Label the darker pairs A and the lighter pairs B.

PIECING

STEP ONE

Join three A squares together and three B squares together (Fig. 2). Sew these to the sides of the large pieced square you have already made (Fig. 3). Press the seams in the same direction as the diagonal seams.

STEP TWO

Join four A squares together with one B square and four B squares together with one A square (Fig. 4). Press the seams in the same direction as the diagonal seams, then sew them to the top and bottom of the set made in step 1 (Fig. 5). Make sixty of these sets.

STEP THREE

Sew four of the sets made in step 2 together, placing the large dark triangle and the single A square towards the centre (Fig. 6). Make fifteen of these sets.

STEP FOUR

Arrange the sets together in five rows of three blocks each on the floor or a large table. Rearrange them until you are satisfied with the effect, then join them to form the quilt top.

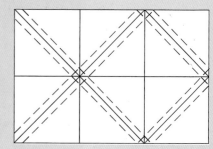

Fig. 1

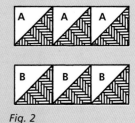

Fig. 2

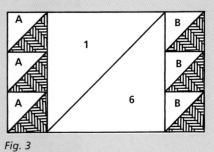

Fig. 3

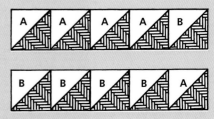

Fig. 4

BORDERS

Measure the length of the quilt top, measuring through the centre. Cut 16.5 cm (6¹/2 in) wide borders to this length and sew them to the quilt sides. Measure, cut and sew the top and bottom borders in the same way. Press the quilt top well.

ASSEMBLING

STEP ONE

Cut the backing fabric in half, then rejoin the pieces to double the width.

STEP TWO

Pin or tape the backing face down on the work surface. Centre the wadding on top. Place the quilt top on top of that, face upwards. Smooth out each layer as you put it down. Secure the layers of the quilt sandwich with the safety pins.

QUILTING

Machine-quilt 'in-the-ditch' along all the outlines of the squares in a grid pattern. Continue the stitching across the borders.

TO FINISH

STEP ONE

Trim the wadding and the backing to the size of the quilt top.

STEP TWO

Cut 9 cm (3¹/2 in) wide strips for the binding. Fold the binding strips over double with the wrong sides together and the raw edges even. Sew the binding to the sides of the quilt with the raw edges even, then to the top and bottom. Turn the folded edge of the binding to the back of the quilt and slipstitch it in place, mitring the corners.

STEP THREE

If you want to hang the quilt, sew a hanging sleeve on the back. See page 153 for how to sew a hanging sleeve.

STEP FOUR

Label your quilt.

HINT

The success of this quilt depends on the contrast between light and dark fabrics. Black or navy provide the strongest dark and this works very well for this quilt. Some fabrics fall naturally into 'light' or 'dark' piles. Others will change their character, depending on their partner fabrics. To help you decide, place the fabrics together, stand back and squint. If the contrast is not sufficient, change one of the fabrics in the pair. Tone-on-tone fabrics add great interest to a quilt and are available in most fabric ranges. Lynne has used these to great effect.

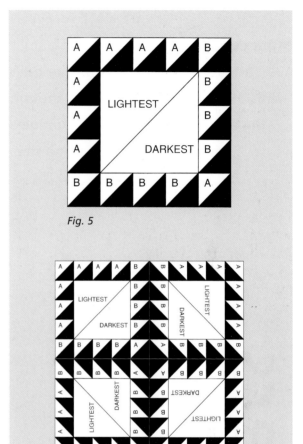

Fig. 5

Fig. 6

A SET OF PIECED BLOCKS

seven sisters

BY KATE McEWEN

Kate decided to make this lovely quilt after she bought an antique quilt which looks very much like it, though the antique quilt has pink triangles and is not quite the same size.

The design is a much-loved traditional one, and a great way to lighten your scrap bag a little. All the stars in the hexagons are made from fabrics with a traditional look. This design also looks very, very nice made up in cotton Liberty prints. The blocks have been set against a pretty, pale blue fabric.

This quilt is machine-pieced and machine-quilted.

FINISHED SIZE

Quilt: 228 cm x 290 cm (90 in x 114 in)
Block size: 51 cm x 46 cm (20 in x 18 in)
Total number of blocks: thirteen full blocks and four part-blocks

FABRIC REQUIREMENTS

Sufficient scrap fabric for 147 stars (one 6.5 cm x 115 cm (2^{1}/$_{2}$ in x 45 in) strip will yield enough diamonds to make two stars)
2 m (2^{1}/$_{4}$ yd) of cream fabric for the background
220 cm (86 in) of blue fabric for the triangles
280 cm (110 in) of blue fabric for the inner and outer borders and the binding
7.2 m (7^{3}/$_{4}$ yd) of fabric for the backing
238 cm x 300 cm (94 in x 118 in) of wadding

OTHER REQUIREMENTS

Quilter's ruler
Pencil
Fineline permanent marker pen
Scissors
Template plastic
Matching sewing thread
Quilting thread
Masking tape
Rotary cutter
Self-healing cutting mat

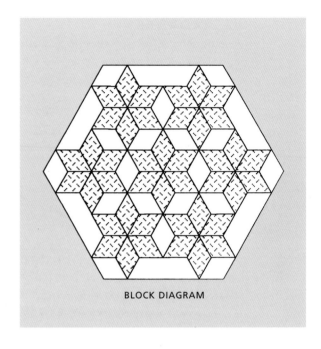

BLOCK DIAGRAM

MAKING THE TEMPLATES

See the templates on page 75.
Note: 7.5 mm (1/4 in) seam allowances are already included in the templates.

Draw around the templates on the back of the fabric. Cut them out on the pencil line. When piecing, place the edge of the presser foot on the cut edge of the fabric. To ensure an exact 7.5 mm (1/4 in) seam allowance, test your sewing machine before you begin (see page 48).

STEP ONE

Using the 60-degree angle on the quilter's ruler, draw a triangle template on the template plastic whose height from the centre of the base to the top point is 24 cm (9^{1}/$_{2}$ in) (Fig. 1). Cut it out.

STEP TWO

Trace the templates M and N onto the template plastic, using the marker pen. Cut them out exactly on the line.

seven sisters

CUTTING

STEP ONE

Using template M, cut six diamonds for each star from the scrap fabrics. If you want to make it a very scrappy quilt, cut each star from a different fabric.

STEP TWO

From the cream fabric, cut the following pieces:
- using template M, cut 136 diamonds; and
- using template N, cut 94 pieces.

STEP THREE

From the blue fabric, cut 24 cm (9¹/₂ in) wide strips, then using the 60-degree triangle, cut the strips into forty triangles, as before.

PIECING

STEP ONE

For each scrap fabric, sew three diamonds together, twice (Fig. 2). Join the six diamonds to make a star. Make seven stars for each hexagonal block in this way.

STEP TWO

Piece the centre of the hexagon blocks by linking the stars with the cream diamonds.

STEP THREE

To complete the block, following the block diagram, sew on the cream N pieces and the cream diamonds at the corners of the hexagon.

STEP FOUR

Join the hexagon blocks together, linking them with the blue triangles as shown in the photograph. Press, then trim the sides so they are even.

BORDERS

STEP ONE

Measure the length of the quilt, measuring through the centre. Cut the strips for the inner border 9 cm (3¹/₂ in) wide by this length. Sew the borders to the sides of the quilt top.

STEP TWO

Measure, cut and sew the top and bottom borders in the same way.

STEP THREE

Make fifty-eight more stars in the same way as for the blocks and sew them together with pieces cut from templates M and N in the cream fabric to make strips for the borders (Fig. 3). Sew these strips to the quilt top in the same way as for the inner borders.

STEP FOUR

Measure, cut and sew the 9 cm (3¹/₂ in) wide outer border from the blue fabric. Press the quilt top.

ONE SEVEN SISTERS BLOCK

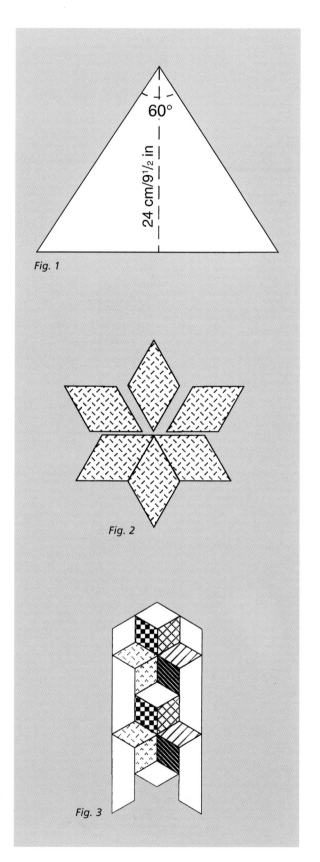

Fig. 1

Fig. 2

Fig. 3

ASSEMBLING

STEP ONE

Cut the backing fabric into thirds, lengthwise, then rejoin the pieces to triple the width. Press the seams open. The seams will run across the back of the quilt.

STEP TWO

Pin or tape the backing face down on the work surface. Centre the wadding on top. Place the completed quilt top, face upwards, on top of the wadding. Smooth out each layer as you put it down. Secure the layers of the quilt sandwich, using the safety pins.

QUILTING

Begin quilting in the centre of the quilt by tightly rolling up the sides of the quilt. Stitch around all the stars in the hexagons, then the hexagons themselves. Then stitch around the borders 'in-the-ditch'. If you wish, you can quilt a graceful design in the plain triangles to add further interest to the quilt.

TO FINISH

STEP ONE

Trim the backing and wadding to the size of the quilt top.

STEP TWO

Cut the binding 9 cm (3½ in) wide by the length and width of the quilt, measuring through the centre of the quilt as before.

STEP THREE

Fold the binding over double with the wrong sides together and with the raw edges even. Sew the binding to the right side of the quilt, with the raw edges even. Sew on all four sides, then turn the folded edge of the binding to the back of the quilt and slipstitch it in place, mitring the corners.

STEP FOUR

Label your quilt.

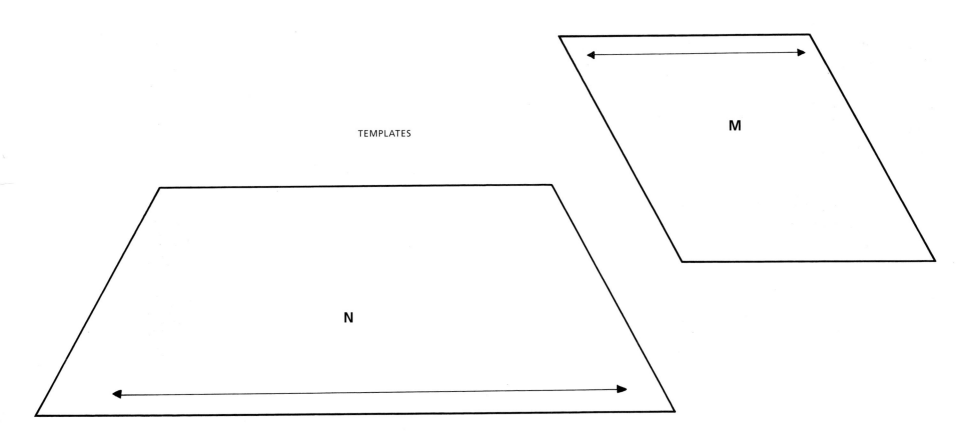

TEMPLATES

BY KATE McEWEN

The right choice of fabric is crucial to the success of this quilt as it relies on careful shade variation to make the pattern.

The dark fabrics should all be of the same value and so should the light fabrics. The design can be best appreciated if the quilt is hung as a wallhanging, rather than if it is spread on a bed.

This quilt is machine-pieced and machine-quilted.

FINISHED SIZE

Quilt: 127 cm x 142 cm (50 in x 56 in)

FABRIC REQUIREMENTS

60 cm (24 in) each of the dark green fabrics, light green fabrics, dark gold fabrics and light gold fabrics

1.5 m (1²/₃ yd) of light gold fabric for the inner border

1.5 m (1²/₃ yd) of dark green fabric for the outer border

2.7 m (3 yd) of fabric for the backing

132 cm x 150 cm (51 in x 60 in) of wadding

45 cm (18 in) of fabric for the binding

OTHER REQUIREMENTS

Quilter's ruler
Template plastic
Rotary cutter
Self-healing cutting mat
Scissors
4 cm (1¹/₂ in) safety pins
Glass-headed pins
Matching sewing thread
Monofilament quilting thread
Masking tape

CUTTING

See the triangle template on page 79.

Note: 7.5 mm (¹/₄ in) seam allowances are included in the measurements.

STEP ONE

Fold each fabric in half selvage to selvage, then fold it in half again. Using the rotary cutter, cut one 9 cm (3¹/₂ in) wide strip across the width of the material from each fabric.

STEP TWO

With the right sides facing, sew two different dark green strips together, along one long edge (Fig. 1).

STEP THREE

Without opening out the two strips, draw 60-degree triangles from the beginning of the strip to the end, using the template (Fig. 2). Some of the triangles (those cut from the sewn side) will be joined together, while those cut from the other side will have a tiny amount of stitching across the top point, which can easily be removed and the triangles used as single triangles (Fig. 3).

STEP FOUR

Sew, then cut all the strips in the same way as in step 3, always putting the light shades of the same colour together and the dark shades of the same colour together.

STEP FIVE

Press open the sewn triangles and pull apart the unsewn triangles (Fig. 4).

thousand pyramids

thousand pyramids

PIECING

STEP ONE

Sew two of the single triangles to each side of the double triangles, keeping light with light and dark with dark. Now you have a larger triangle, made up of four smaller triangles. Make the same set of triangles out of each colourway, mixing the fabrics but always keeping the dark fabrics together and the light fabrics together.

STEP TWO

Sew the sets made in step 1 together, with the dark green triangles on top of the light green triangles and the dark gold triangles on top of the light gold triangles to form a large pieced diamond (Fig. 5).

STEP THREE

Lay out the triangles made in step 2 on the floor until you have a pleasing design, using the photograph as your guide. Sew the large triangles together in diagonal strips (Fig. 6). Reserve some half-triangle sets for squaring off the top and the bottom of the quilt.

STEP FOUR

Stitch the strips together to form the quilt top, joining in the half-triangle sets as necessary. Trim the sides to be level – you will have to cut through some triangles to achieve this. Press the quilt top when it is completed.

BORDERS

STEP ONE

Cut the 6.5 cm (2$\frac{1}{2}$ in) wide inner border from the light gold fabric. Measure the length of the quilt top, measuring through the centre. Cut the side borders to this length. Sew on the side borders.

STEP TWO

Measure, cut and sew the top and bottom inner borders in the same way.

STEP THREE

Measure, cut and sew the 11.5 cm (4$\frac{1}{2}$ in) wide outer borders from the dark green fabric in the same way as for the inner borders.

ASSEMBLING

STEP ONE

Cut the backing fabric in half widthwise, then rejoin the pieces to achieve the required width.

STEP TWO

Pin or tape the backing face down on the work surface. Centre the wadding on top. Place the quilt top on top of that, face upwards. Smooth out each layer as you put it down. Secure the layers of the quilt sandwich with the safety pins.

QUILTING

Use the monofilament thread through the needle and ordinary sewing thread on the bobbin of the sewing machine. Outline-stitch along the lines that make the pyramid shape, then sew around the borders 'in-the-ditch'.

CLOSE-UP OF THE PIECING

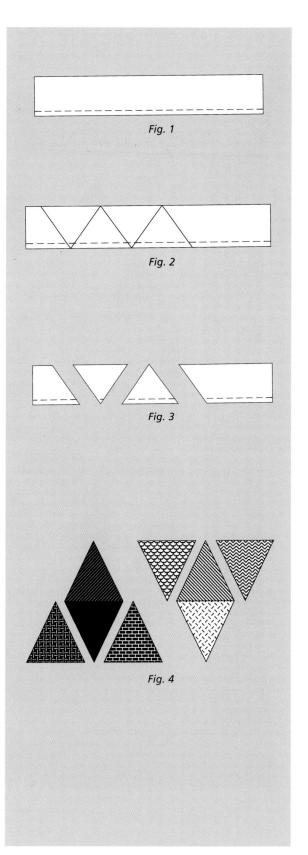

Fig. 1

Fig. 2

Fig. 3

Fig. 4

TO FINISH

STEP ONE

Trim the backing and the wadding to the size of the quilt top.

STEP TWO

Cut out five 9 cm (3¼ in) wide strips for the binding from the binding fabric. Use the fifth strip to lengthen the other four to achieve the required length.

STEP THREE

Fold the binding fabric over double with the wrong sides together and the raw edges even. Sew the binding to the right side of the quilt with the raw edges even. When all four bindings are attached, turn them on to the back of the quilt and slipstitch them in place, mitring the corners.

STEP FOUR

If you want to hang the quilt, sew a sleeve on the back of the quilt to pass a rod through. See page 153 for how to sew a hanging sleeve.

STEP FIVE

Label your quilt.

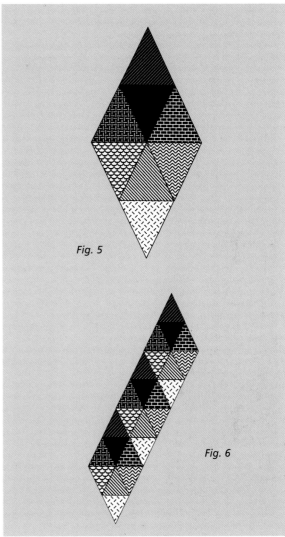

Fig. 5

Fig. 6

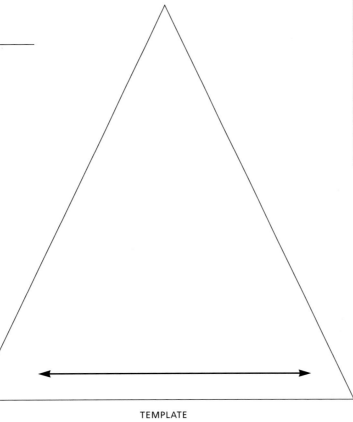

TEMPLATE

appliqué

Appliqué has a very long history. Applying one fabric over another has been used for function and decoration for centuries. Since the nineteenth century, quilts featuring appliqué have become very popular and today we can enjoy a wide range of styles, all stemming from that tradition.

Appliqué is a method of applying one fabric over another. Traditionally, this has been done with tiny, almost invisible hand-stitches, but examples of naive appliqué often have quite large stitches. Sometimes the very stitches become an integral element of the design.

Examples of appliqué that are many, many hundreds of years old can be seen in museums. In medieval times, appliqué was used extensively to furnish the homes of the well-to-do, often in the form of decorative hangings on walls, doorways – even around beds.

Appliquéd quilts were seen from the nineteenth century onwards and became most popular in the United States. The most celebrated form was the Album quilt, comprising a number of different, beautifully executed appliqué blocks. These were made to mark special occasions, such as weddings; for friendship or patriotism; or as gestures of thanks or goodwill. The most famous of these quilt styles was the Baltimore quilt, which featured glorious wreaths, baskets of flowers, garlands and the like. Today, flowers are still the most popular appliqué motif, but quiltmakers show great imagination and daring with appliqué quilts featuring animals, buildings, portraits, food – in fact, just about any motif is considered suitable.

Appliqué can be sewn by hand or by machine. Both methods are popular.

PREPARING FOR APPLIQUE
PREPARING THE BLOCK

Where the appliqué pieces are worked on a background square, you will need to cut these pieces out first, at the size given in the instructions. If the appliqué needs to be centred on the background square, fold it into quarters and finger-press the fold to find the centre.

When you have prepared the templates (see page 83), place them on the right side of the background and lightly draw around them with a water-soluble marker pen, made specifically for the purpose, or a soft pencil. Use a light touch for all marking. If you are using the marker pen, test that it will wash out of the fabric properly. If there are two or more layers to the appliqué, it is only necessary to mark the bottom layer.

It is usually a good idea to cut the appliqué pieces for one block at a time.

Many appliqué designs have pieces overlapping one another at various points. Look closely at the picture and the pattern to work out the order in which to proceed with the appliqué, so you can begin with the bottom piece. Where there are flower stems, take care that the raw end of the stem is hidden under the leaf or flower.

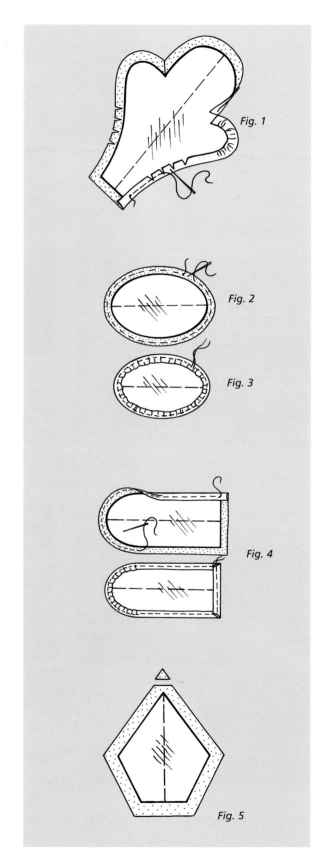

Fig. 1

Fig. 2

Fig. 3

Fig. 4

Fig. 5

PREPARING APPLIQUE PIECES

Pre-basting method

This method gives a crisp outline to the appliqué and a high degree of accuracy.

Trace the templates onto template plastic or cardboard and cut them out exactly on the line. These are the master templates. Using the master templates, cut out the shape from lightweight cardboard for each piece to be appliquéd. Manilla folders are ideal.

Place the fabric, face down on a sandpaper board. This will help to hold the fabric in place while you trace around the template. Cut out the fabric with a 5 mm (scant 1/4 in) seam allowance all around.

Clip into any curves or corners. Place the cardboard shape on the wrong side of the fabric. Baste the fabric and the cardboard down the middle. Trim any excess seam allowance from the points. Turn the seam allowances over the cardboard and baste them in place, stitching through the seam allowance and the cardboard. (Fig. 1). Press the piece carefully with a little spray starch for a very crisp finish. Remove the basting and the cardboard. Your shape is now ready to appliqué.

For perfect circles or ovals, such as for the centres of flowers, cut a fabric circle the finished size plus 1.5 cm (1/2 in). Run a gathering stitch close to the edge. Centre the cardboard circle on the wrong side of the fabric and baste them together, down the middle (Fig. 2). Pull up the gathering tightly and secure the thread (Fig. 3). Press well, using the point of the iron to press the seam allowance flat. This method for dealing with curves can be used on any curved appliqué (Fig. 4).

To deal with sharp points, prepare the cardboard shapes and cut out the fabric as before. Baste the cardboard to the wrong side of the fabric, down the middle. Trim the fabric from the points. Baste up to the point, fold in and stitch the fullness at the point, then continue basting the other side (Figs 5 – 8).

When basting around the top of a heart shape, clip into the V at the top and spread the seam allowance so it lies flat (Fig. 9).

Finger- or needleturn method

This method is quicker, but is not as accurate for the less experienced quiltmaker. However, with practice, many quiltmakers achieve excellent results and it becomes their preferred method.

Trace the templates onto template plastic and cut them out. Place the fabric, face up, on the sandpaper board. Position the template and draw around it. Note that you are marking the right side of the fabric. Cut out each piece with a 4 mm (3/16 in) seam allowance.

Pin and/or baste the appliqué piece into position on the right side of the background fabric. Starting at a relatively straight edge, use your fingers or the shank of the needle to roll the seam allowance under, just hiding the marked sewing line and secure it with a few tiny stitches (Fig. 10).

Freezer paper method

Freezer paper offers a relatively new method of hand-appliqué. Note this is a special kind of freezer paper, available in patchwork shops. It can be used on top of the appliqué piece as a stabiliser, which is removed, or under the appliqué piece to attach it to the background.

In the first method, trace the appliqué onto the matte side of the freezer paper. Cut it out without seam allowances to use as the template. Place the template onto the right side of the fabric, then press with a medium-hot, dry iron. Cut out the piece, adding 4 mm (3/16 in) seam allowances. Pin, then baste the piece onto the background. Appliqué the piece into place, turning under the seam allowances, using the needleturn method. When the stitching is completed, remove the basting and the freezer paper.

In the second freezer paper method, trace the appliqué onto the matte side of the freezer paper. Cut it out without seam allowances to use as a template. Place the template, reversed, on the wrong side of the fabric, shiny side up. Trace around the motif, then cut it out adding 6 mm (1/4 in) seam allowances all around. It is a good idea to trim the seam allowance right back on any inward curves to make the next step easier. Position the template, shiny side up, on the wrong side of the fabric and, using a hot, dry iron, press the seam allowances over the freezer paper. Next, place the appliqué piece in position on the background and fuse it into place. To remove the freezer paper, turn the block over and cut a small slit in the background fabric, under the appliquéd motif. Carefully pull the freezer paper out through the slit. Tweezers can be helpful if the space is very small. Slipstitch the opening closed.

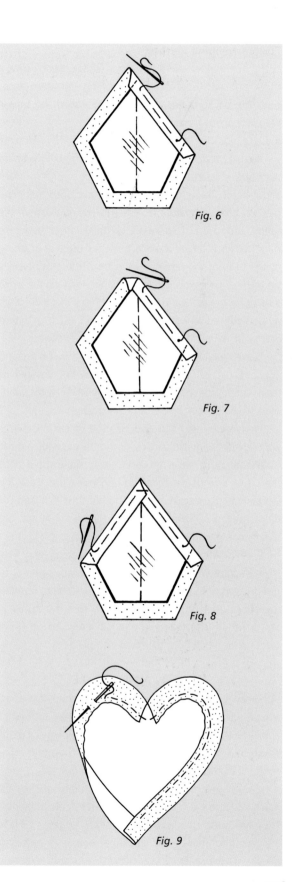

Fig. 6

Fig. 7

Fig. 8

Fig. 9

Fusible webbing method

Many quiltmakers use lightweight fusible webbing as a quick and easy method for attaching appliqué pieces onto the background. Unlike freezer paper, the fusible webbing is not removed. Once the piece has been fixed in place, you can stitch around it by hand or by machine.

Fusible webbing is most commonly used to prepare appliqué shapes which are cut out without seam allowances. Trace the appliqué motif onto template plastic. Draw around the template on the right side of the fabric and cut out a square, slightly larger than the pattern (Fig. 11). Fuse a similarly shaped piece of webbing to the back of the fabric, then cut out the motif exactly on the line. Remove the backing paper and fuse the piece into place on the background. To finish, machine-stitch around the edge with a machine satin stitch or hand-stitch a small chain stitch, covering the raw edge.

Naive appliqué can also use fusible webbing and appliqué cut without seam allowances but, instead of satin stitch, the pieces are often finished with hand-worked, bold, buttonhole or chain stitch.

Fusible webbing can also be used where the pieces are cut with seam allowances, giving the appliqué a more traditional look. Trace the reversed appliqué motif onto the paper side of the webbing and cut it out. Fuse the webbing in place on the wrong side of the fabric and cut it out, adding 7.5 mm (1/4 in) seam allowances all around. Clip into curves and corners. Remove the backing, then turn the seam allowance onto the webbing and fuse them in place with the point of the iron. Take care not to run the iron onto the sticky side of the webbing. Position the appliqué on the background and fuse it into place. This method still leaves the edges free, so you can slipstitch or machine-stitch them into place.

HAND-APPLIQUE

Hand-sewn appliqué is the traditional method. It uses an almost invisible stitch, but is slower than machine-appliqué. Beginners will find it easier to appliqué a motif which has few sharp curves. As you become more confident, progress to more complex shapes.

Choose one hundred per cent cotton fabrics. They are much easier to work with than polyester or blend fabrics. They will press cleanly with nice sharp edges, which is important for pre-basted appliqué, and it is easier to needleturn the seam allowances with pure cotton fabrics.

There are several methods described here for hand-appliqué. Choose the one which best suits you and the look you are trying to achieve. You can mix methods, pre-basting difficult shapes and needleturning for others.

Generally, choose a thread to match the appliqué, unless you want the stitching to be a feature, such as in 'A Little Bit of Love' on page 90.

HAND-APPLIQUE STITCHES

The most common way to hand-sew the appliqué piece to the background fabric is using small stitches that are very close together, just catching a few threads of the fabric (Fig. 12). Some quilters use a tiny chain stitch which is worked right on the edge of the appliqué piece, but generally reserve this for appliqué with fusible webbing (Fig. 13). A running stitch or blanket stitch can also be used (Fig. 14).

MACHINE-APPLIQUE

Appliqué by machine is quick and very effective, using a satin stitch, blind hem stitch or a simple straight stitch.

SATIN-STITCH APPLIQUE

It is a good idea to test the satin stitch on a practice piece first to determine the length and width of stitches that look best. The wider the stitches, the more prominent the stitching will be, so decide if you want to make it a feature or not.

Prepare and mark the background fabric. Because a close satin stitch covers and protects the edge of the appliqué, you can cut these pieces out without seam allowances. Pin, baste or fuse them to the background, starting with the piece that is on the bottom, closest to the background.

To protect the background from distortion, some quiltmakers like to stabilise the area behind the appliqué, before they begin satin stitching. You can use a stabiliser that is torn away after the stitching is completed, or use a lightweight interfacing which stays in place. Decide what sort of feel you would like your quilt to have – interfacing is naturally firmer.

For pinned or basted appliqué, stitch around the piece first, using a straight stitch or a medium zigzag stitch, then set your sewing machine for satin stitch and stitch over the first line of stitches, covering them and the edge of the fabric.

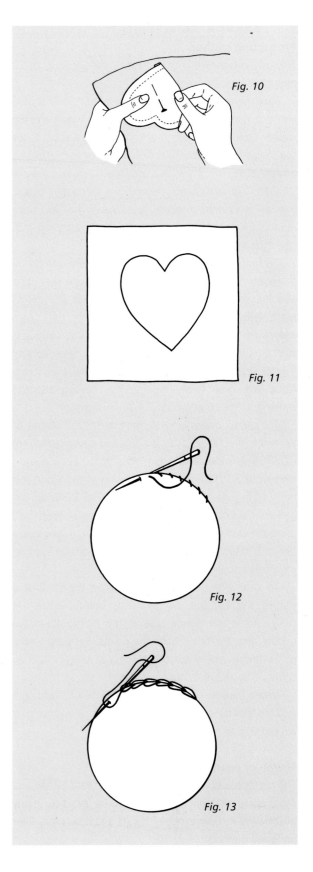

Fig. 10

Fig. 11

Fig. 12

Fig. 13

Stitch slowly, guiding the machine around the curves. To stitch curves, stop the machine frequently leaving the needle in the fabric and turning the block to ensure a smooth line of stitches.

For corners, stitch up to the corner, then stop, leaving the needle in the outside edge. Turn the block and continue sewing so the first few stitches cover the previous stitches (Fig. 15).

For points, such as the ends of leaves, stitch up to the point, tapering the stitches as you get close to it. At the point, leave the needle in the fabric and pivot the fabric, then continue stitching, gradually increasing the size of the stitches as you work away from the point (Fig. 16).

BLIND HEM-STITCH APPLIQUE

If you have a sewing machine that can do a blind hem stitch, this method produces an almost invisible stitch. Practise on a test piece first to determine the needle and foot positions. The idea is to produce a stitch which runs alongside the piece to be appliquéd and every few stitches takes a little stitch to the left, catching the appliqué piece (Fig. 17).

Use a monofilament thread for this stitch and make appropriate adjustments to the tension and the threading of your sewing machine (see page 154).

STRAIGHT-STITCH APPLIQUE

Straight stitch is the simplest of all stitches on the sewing machine. Prepare and mark the background. Prepare the appliqué pieces, using one of the methods already described. For this type of appliqué it is essential to cut out the appliqué pieces with a seam allowance, then pin-baste or fuse them into place.

Set the stitch length to five or six to a centimetre (twelve to fourteen to the inch) and install an open-toed embroidery foot. This type of foot gives you an unobstructed view of the stitching line, which is very helpful in guiding your work. Stitch very close to the folded edge of the appliqué, beginning and ending on a straight edge.

REDUCING BULK

Whichever method of appliqué you choose, it is important to remove any excess bulk. This is particularly true where a number of fabrics have been layered on top of one another.

When all the appliqué is completed, turn the block over and using a sharp pair of scissors cut away the background fabric and any other unnecessary layers. Take great care not to cut through the top layer.

STEMS AND VINES

Many appliqué designs include narrow pieces, such as stems and vines. As there is a special method for preparing these, it is worth dealing with them separately.

If the design uses straight stems, they can be cut on the straight grain of the fabric. If, however, the stems or vines are curved, you will need to cut them on the bias, so they can be gently curved into the appropriate shape.

If you only need a short length of bias strip, cut out a square of fabric and fold it in half diagonally. Press the fold. Open out the square and, using the pressed line as your guide, cut strips of the desired width.

If you need long lengths of bias, prepare them using the method described for continuous bias binding on page 153.

PREPARING STEMS OR VINES

Cut a bias strip that is three times wider than the required finished width. Fold one raw edge to the centre, fold the other raw edge over it, ending just short of the fold. Press carefully. Do not push and pull with the iron. This will stretch the bias strip.

Alternatively, cut the bias strip twice the desired finished width plus 1.5 cm (1/2 in) for seam allowances. Fold the strip over double with the right sides together and stitch in a 7.5 mm (1/4 in) seam. Turn the strip to the right side and roll it so the seam is at the centre back. Carefully press the strip.

You can also use bias folders which are available in various widths from haberdashery shops. Cut the bias strip and feed it into one end of the appropriately sized bias folder. Do this on your ironing board so you can press the prepared bias binding as it comes out of the other end of the bias folder.

Bias pressing bars can be very useful in ensuring a crisp edge to your bias strips. These are sold in various widths and can be bought at patchwork shops and haberdashery departments.

Appliqué the stem or vine in place using your preferred appliqué method.

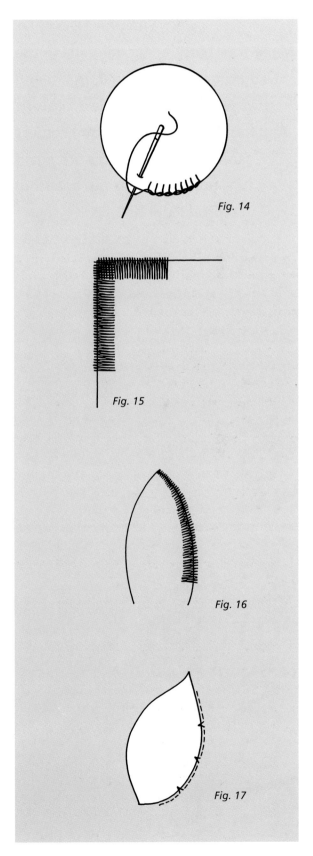

Fig. 14

Fig. 15

Fig. 16

Fig. 17

flowers for georgia

BY SANDRA EDWARDS

Many four-block appliqué quilts in the traditional colours of red, green and gold were made in the last century. Appliquéd quilts using strong colours and large-scale pieces are again popular, using the beautiful reproduction fabrics which are available today.

Sandra has used a very modern method of appliqué for this quilt, which utilises freezer paper. This gives a very neat result with a minimum of effort. For more information about appliqué with freezer paper, see page 83.

This quilt is machine-appliquéd and machine-quilted.

FINISHED SIZE

Quilt: 130 cm (50 in) square
Block size: 50 cm (20 in)
Total number of blocks: Four

FABRIC REQUIREMENTS

1.6 m (1³/4 yd) of fabric for the background
1.15 m (1¹/8 yd) of red fabric for the border triangles
50 cm (¹/2 yd) of green fabric for the leaves and stems
50 cm (¹/2 yd) in total of assorted gold fabrics
25 cm (¹/4 yd) of red fabric
25 cm (¹/4 yd) of dark red fabric
25 cm (¹/4 yd) of burgundy fabric
50 cm (¹/2 yd) of fabric for the binding
2.2 m (2¹/4 yd) of fabric for the backing
140 cm x 140 cm (54 in x 54 in) of wadding

OTHER REQUIREMENTS

Template plastic
Freezer paper
Monofilament thread
Rotary cutter
Quilter's ruler
Self-healing cutting mat
Bobbinfil thread to match the background fabric
Glue stick suitable for fabric
Black fineline marker pen
Pencil
Usual sewing supplies
Masking tape
Safety pins

APPLIQUE

See the templates and the appliqué pattern on Pull Out Pattern Sheet 2. Note that the templates do not include the seam allowances. Add 3 mm (¹/8 in) as you cut them out of fabric.

STEP ONE

From the background fabric, cut four 53.5 cm (20¹/2 in) squares.

STEP TWO

Measure the lengths required for the stems and cut 3 cm (1¹/4 in) wide bias strips from the green fabric to these lengths plus allowances. Fold the strips over double with the wrong sides facing. Sew the raw edges together with a 3 mm (¹/8 in) seam allowance. Insert a 12 mm (¹/2 in) bias bar into each tube. Press the stem carefully, turning the seam allowance to the underside. Remove the bias bar. Using the iron, you can gently curve the bias stems in the directions shown in the photograph..

STEP THREE

Appliqué the stems onto the background fabric, using the photograph and pattern as a guide. Sew the pieces into place by machine with a small blind hemming stitch or zigzag stitch, using the monofilament thread in the top of the machine and the Bobbinfil in the bobbin.

STEP FOUR

Trace and cut out a plastic template for each appliqué piece of the vase, flowers and leaves. Trace around each template on the dull side of the freezer paper, using the pencil. Cut out each shape smoothly and carefully on the pencil line.

STEP FIVE

Iron each freezer paper shape onto the back of the appropriate appliqué fabric. Cut out each shape, leaving a 3 mm (¹/8 in) seam allowance.

flowers for georgia

STEP SIX

Using the glue stick, apply a little glue to the seam allowance. Stick the seam allowance onto the back of the freezer paper.

STEP SEVEN

Position the appliqué pieces on the background. Sew them into place by machine with a small blind hemming stitch or zigzag stitch, using the monofilament thread in the top of the machine and the Bobbinfil in the bobbin. From the back, cut away the background fabric behind the appliqué pieces with small sharp scissors leaving a 7.5 mm (1/4 in) seam allowance.

STEP EIGHT

From the back of the work, spray the seam allowance with a little water to release the glue and enable you to remove the freezer paper. Dry your appliqué quickly, using a hair dryer or iron on the back. Make four blocks in the same way.

ASSEMBLING

Sew the blocks together with a 7.5 mm (1/4 in) seam allowance to complete the centre of the quilt.

BORDERS

Note: Seam allowances of 7.5 mm (1/4 in) are included in the measurements for the borders.

STEP ONE

From the background fabric cut four strips of fabric 10.75 cm (4^1/$_{16}$ in) wide, cutting across the width of the fabric. Cut the strips into thirty-six 10.75 cm (4^1/$_{16}$ in) squares (A).

STEP TWO

From the red fabric cut one strip of fabric 9 cm (3^3/$_8$ in) wide. Cut it into eight 9 cm (3^3/$_8$ in) squares. Cut the squares in half diagonally, once, to yield sixteen half-square triangles (B).

STEP THREE

From the red fabric, cut three 16.5 cm (6^1/$_4$ in) wide strips. Cut the strips into sixteen 16.5 cm (6^1/$_4$ in) squares. Cut the squares in half diagonally, twice, to yield sixty-four quarter-square triangles (C).

STEP FOUR

Following figure 1, sew two C triangles to an A square. Press the seam allowances towards the square. Make six of these units for each side border. Add two B triangles to the last C/A unit on each end (Fig. 2). Sew the units together to complete the side borders.

STEP FIVE

Make eight C/A/C units for the top and bottom borders. Add two B triangles to the last C/A unit on each end. Sew the units together to complete the top and bottom borders of the quilt.

STEP SIX

Sew the side borders to the quilt top, then add the top and bottom borders to complete the quilt top (Fig. 3).

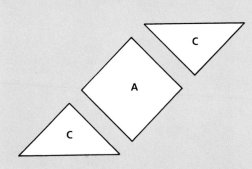

Fig. 1

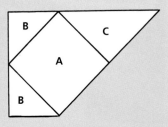

Fig. 2

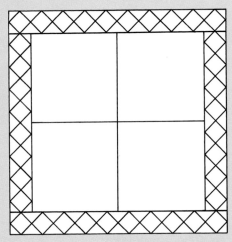

Fig. 3

TO FINISH

STEP ONE

Mark the quilting design onto the quilt top. Sandra has quilted a 5 cm (2 in) grid over the entire background. All the appliqué pieces have been quilted as have the squares in the pieced border.

STEP TWO

Pin or tape the backing face down on the work surface. Centre the wadding on top. Place the quilt top on top of that, face upwards. Smooth out each layer as you put it down. Pin or baste to secure the layers.

STEP THREE

Quilt as desired. Sandra has machine-quilted her quilt, using monofilament thread in the patterns described above. She has also quilted 'in-the-ditch' around the borders.

STEP FOUR

Cut six 6 cm (2½ in) wide strips from the binding fabric. Cut the end of each strip at an angle of forty-five degrees. Join the strips end-to-end. Fold the strip double, lengthwise, with the wrong sides together and raw edges matching. Press. Sew the binding to the right side of the quilt top with all the raw edges matching. Mitre the corners as you turn the binding to the back of the quilt and slipstitch it in place by hand.

STEP FIVE

If your quilt is to be hung, make a sleeve for passing the rod through. See page 153 for how to make a hanging sleeve.

THE APPLIQUE BLOCK

APPLIQUE WITH A SMALL BLIND-HEM STITCH

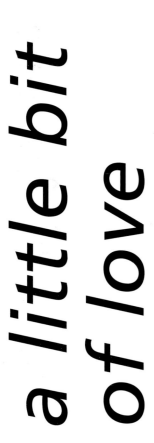

BY YOLANDA GIFFORD

This wonderful quilt takes its name from a large bed quilt of eighty blocks, which Yolanda made and called 'The Love Quilt'. 'A Little Bit of Love' is a smaller version, but loses nothing of the colour and vibrancy of its larger sibling.

Composed of twelve blocks, the quilt features simple motifs appliquéd in a naive fashion on ten of the twelve blocks; the remaining two blocks are plain – if that word can be used to describe a bright purple print!

Yolanda recommends that you read all the instructions, before commencing the quilt.

This quilt is hand-appliquéd, machine-pieced and hand-quilted.

FINISHED SIZE

Quilt: 100 cm x 115 cm (39 in x 45 in)
Block size: 20 cm (8 in)
Total number of blocks: twelve

FABRIC REQUIREMENTS

Twelve brightly coloured 20 cm (8 in) squares of
  fabric for the backgrounds
Assortment of bright fabrics for the appliqué
25 cm (1/4 yd) of fusible webbing
100 cm x 115 cm (39 in x 45 in) of wadding
12 cm (5 in) of fabric for the inner border
80 cm (32 in) of fabric for the outer border
40 cm (16 in) of fabric for the binding
1 m (1 1/4 yd) of fabric for the backing

OTHER REQUIREMENTS

Embroidery thread in six different colours
25 cm (1/4 yd) each of red and yellow rickrack braid
Cotton threads for the appliqué
Large button
Crewel needle, size 7
Small hand-sewing needle
Cardboard
Black fineline permanent marker pen
Pencil
Usual sewing supplies

APPLIQUE

See the patterns on pages 93–97. Note that seam allowances of 1 cm (1/2 in) are included in the block and strip measurements. Add a 7.5 mm (1/4 in) seam allowance when cutting the appliqué pieces from the fabric.

STEP ONE

Trace the patterns and transfer each element of them to the cardboard. Label each piece. Cut them out exactly on the line. These will be the templates.

STEP TWO

Lay out the twelve background squares, establishing their position in the quilt. Choose the ten blocks which will be appliquéd.

STEP THREE

For the flower block, trace the pattern onto the smooth side of the fusible webbing, using the pencil. Cut out a rough square around the tracing. Fuse the webbing to the wrong side of the appliqué fabrics, then cut out exactly on the pencil line.

STEP FOUR

Using the pencil, draw around the templates on the front of the chosen appliqué fabrics. Cut them out 7.5 mm (1/4 in) outside the pencil line.

STEP FIVE

Appliqué the motifs (except for the flower) onto the nine blocks, using a small slipstitch and turning under the seam allowance up to the pencil line as you go. Choose a thread colour which matches the appliqué.

STEP SIX

For the flower block, peel off the paper backing of the webbing and place the elements face down in the centre of the block. Fuse them into place with a hot iron, beginning with the stem, then the petals, then the flower centre. Using two strands of matching embroidery thread and a small needle, chain stitch around the edges of the appliqué motifs.

a little bit of love

a little bit of love

EMBELLISHING

STEP ONE

Stem stitch the bird's legs in six strands of embroidery cotton. Outline the fabric beneath the fish and the yellow tree with a running stitch, using four strands of cotton. Overstitch the small tree and the patches, using six strands of cotton. Backstitch the features on the sun, using two strands of cotton.

STEP TWO

Sew a button on the basket. Sew on the rickrack braid.

ASSEMBLING

STEP ONE

When all the appliqué is completed, join the blocks into four rows of three, then join the rows to complete the quilt centre.

STEP TWO

From the fabric for the inner border, cut four strips 4 cm (1 1/2 in) wide across the width of the fabric. Sew them to the top and bottom of the quilt, trim the excess, then sew on the side borders.

STEP THREE

From the outer border fabric, cut four strips 20 cm (8 in) wide across the width of the fabric. Sew them to the top and bottom of the quilt, trim, then sew them to the sides.

STEP FOUR

Pin or baste the backing fabric, face down, on the work surface. Centre the wadding on top. Place the quilt top on top of that, face upwards. Smooth out all the layers as you put them down. Pin or baste through all the layers to secure them.

TO FINISH

STEP ONE

Trim the top and the wadding to the size of the backing.

STEP TWO

Cut five binding strips 10 cm (4 in) wide across the width of the fabric. Join them to make one long strip. Press the strip over double with the wrong sides facing. Sew the binding to the right side of the quilt top and bottom, with all the raw edges matching. Trim. Sew the binding to the sides in the same way. Turn the binding to the back of the quilt and slipstitch it into place .

STEP THREE

Outline-quilt around each of the twelve blocks, 12 cm (1/2 in) from the seam, using two strands of cotton. Quilt outside the inner border in the same way.

STEP FOUR

Make a hanging sleeve so that your quilt can be displayed. For more information on how to make a hanging sleeve, see page 153.

STEP FIVE

Label your quilt.

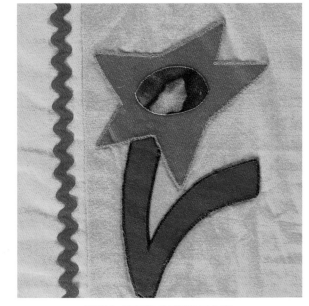

DETAIL OF THE FLOWER BLOCK

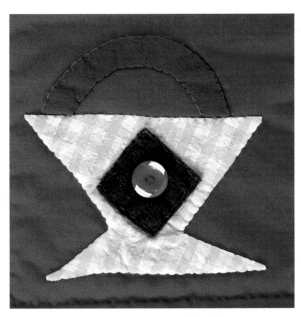

DETAIL OF THE BASKET BLOCK

APPLIQUE PATTERN

APPLIQUE PATTERNS

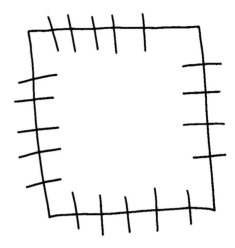

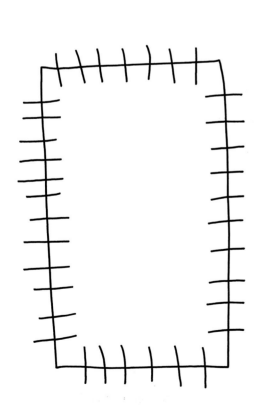

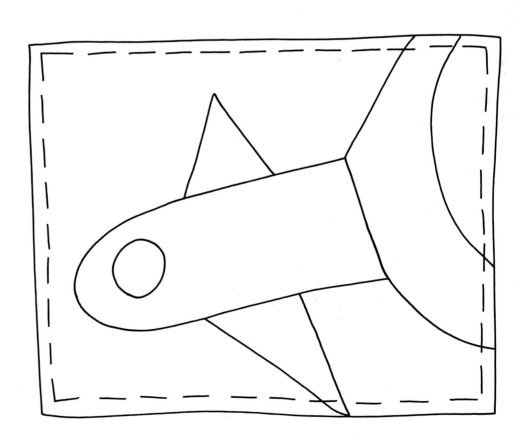

APPLIQUE PATTERNS

APPLIQUE PATTERNS

APPLIQUE PATTERNS

flower garden

BY KATE McEWEN

This is a traditional appliquéd quilt made in a not-so-traditional way. It has been machine-appliquéd, using an invisible thread and a technique that really does look like hand-appliqué – especially after it is quilted.

Quilting around the flower outlines makes them stand out very clearly.

To give this quilt a very dramatic note, Kate has used rusty red and pink flowers and green leaves on a black background. You could make it with a more traditional cream background or with different colours for the appliqué. Shades of blue on a cream background would be very effective.

This quilt is machine-appliquéd and machine-quilted.

FINISHED SIZE

Quilt: 203 cm x 259 cm (80 in x 102 in)
Block size: 41 cm (16 in) square
Total number of blocks: twelve

FABRIC REQUIREMENTS

30 cm (12 in) of rusty red fabric
1.6 m (1³/4 yd) of pink fabric
150 cm (60 in) of green fabric
5 m (5¹/2 yd) of black fabric for the background
5.2 m (5³/4 yd) of fabric for the backing
80 cm (32 in) of fabric for the binding
210 cm x 266 cm (83 in x 105 in) of wadding

OTHER REQUIREMENTS

Quilter's ruler
Transfer paper
Pencil
Glass-headed pins
Tweezers (optional)
Scissors
Freezer paper
Matching sewing thread
Monofilament thread for the quilting and appliqué
Sewing machine with blind hem-stitch foot
Open-toed embroidery foot (optional)
4 cm (1¹/2 in) safety pins
Masking tape
Note: The special freezer paper used for quilting is available in quilt shops. It is waxed on one side and plain on the other, can be ironed on and gives a stiff edge to the appliqué piece.

CUTTING

See the appliqué templates on Pull Out Pattern Sheet 1. Note that the templates do not include seam allowances; add 7.5 mm (¹/4 in) seam allowances to each fabric piece, as you cut it out.

STEP ONE

Cut out twelve 42 cm (16¹/2 in) squares from the background fabric.

STEP TWO

Fold one corner of the green fabric up at an angle of 45 degrees. Cut along the fold to establish the bias. Working from this cut edge, cut plenty of 3 cm (1¹/4 in) wide bias strips for the stalks and the circular wreath.

STEP THREE

Cut twenty-four 7.5 cm (3 in) squares from the pink fabric for the buds.

STEP FOUR

Trace the appliqué templates onto the freezer paper. You will need a separate pattern piece for each piece of appliqué. Trace and cut out from the freezer paper six large inner flowers, six large outer flowers, twenty-four bud bases, 168 leaves and twenty-four small flowers. You will also need to cut flowers and leaves for the borders.

STEP FIVE

Iron each freezer paper pattern piece onto the back of the appropriately coloured fabric. Cut the shape out of the fabric, leaving a 7.5 mm (¹/4 in) seam allowance on the fabric all around. Clip into the curves of the pattern pieces, where necessary.

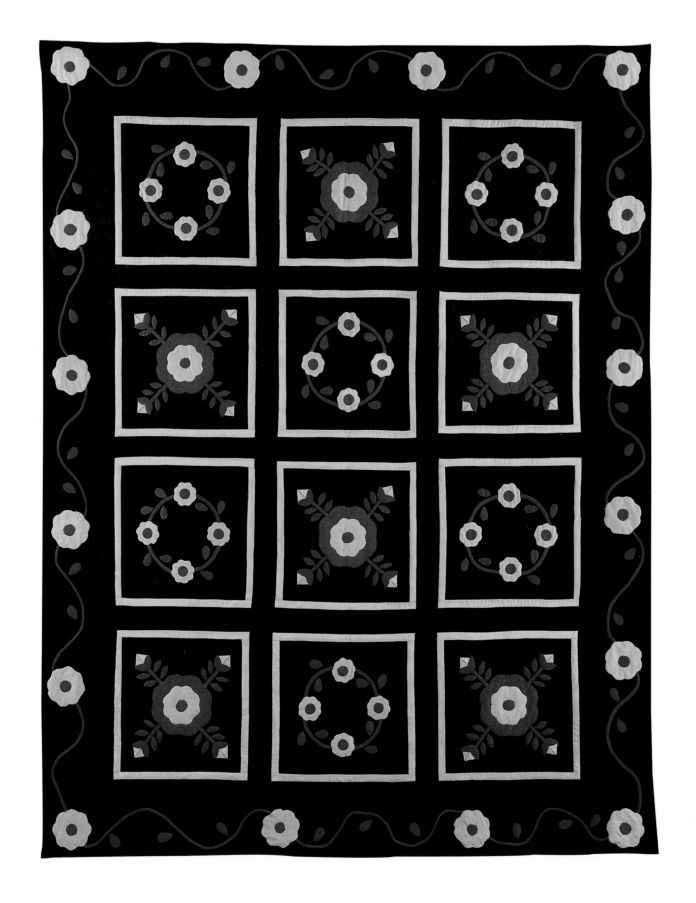

flower garden

APPLIQUE

STEP ONE

You can baste the seam allowance under all around the pattern pieces or you can iron it over the freezer paper. Try both, to find the method that best suits you. Prepare all the pieces for one block in this way.

STEP TWO

To form the folded buds, fold each pink square in half, diagonally. Fold down the two upper points of the triangle to the third point (Figs 1–3).

STEP THREE

Press under 7.5 mm (1/4 in) on the raw long edges of the stem pieces.

STEP FOUR

Fold the background square into quarters and finger-press to find and mark the centre point. Place the appliqué pieces onto the square and pin them in place, beginning with the stems. Take note of any pieces that are overlapped by others – make sure they are in place first. Pin the stem pieces on before the flowers, noting that they can be curved quite easily by gently pressing them into a curved shape with the iron.

STEP FIVE

Set up your sewing machine for appliqué. Use the monofilament thread through the needle and an ordinary sewing thread on the bobbin. Select the blind hem-stitch on your machine and adjust the width of the stitch down to about 1 (or as small as it will go, depending on your machine). If you have one, install the open-toed embroidery foot and adjust the stitch length to about 1/2. Take no notice if your machine tells you to use a blind hem-stitch foot.

STEP SIX

Try this appliqué method on a fabric scrap first. The idea is to stitch on the background, as close as possible to the piece to be appliquéd so that when the machine is straight stitching, the stitching is very close to the piece being appliquéd, and when the machine does the little stitch to the left, it just catches the piece being appliquéd (Fig. 4). Sew all around the piece, then do a couple of backstitches to secure it and go on to the next piece.

That is all there is to it, but it does take a bit of trial and error with the stitch width to get it just right. If the bobbin thread is pulling up, loosen the top tension a bit.

For more information about this method of appliqué, see page 85.

STEP SEVEN

When you have appliquéd all the blocks, cut a small slit in the background fabric behind the appliqué and gently pull out the freezer paper. Tweezers can make this easier to do.

PIECING

STEP ONE

Cut 4 cm (1 1/2 in) wide strips for the frames around the blocks from the pink fabric. Sew on the side frames first, then the top and bottom frames. Press all the blocks.

STEP TWO

Cut 9 cm (3 1/2 in) wide sashing strips from the background fabric. Join five blocks vertically with a length of sashing between them and a length at the top and the bottom. Make three of these sets.

STEP THREE

Measure the length of the sets formed in step 2 and cut four pieces of sashing to this length. Join the three sets together with a length of sashing in between.

BORDERS

STEP ONE

Measure the length of the quilt top, measuring through the centre. Cut 16.5 cm (6 1/2 in) wide side borders to this length. Sew the side borders to the side edges of the quilt. Measure, cut and sew the top and bottom borders in the same way.

STEP TWO

Cut some more green bias strips as before and pin them in place, curving them around along the border. Add leaves and flowers as you like and appliqué all the elements in place as before. When you have finished the quilt top, press it well on the wrong side.

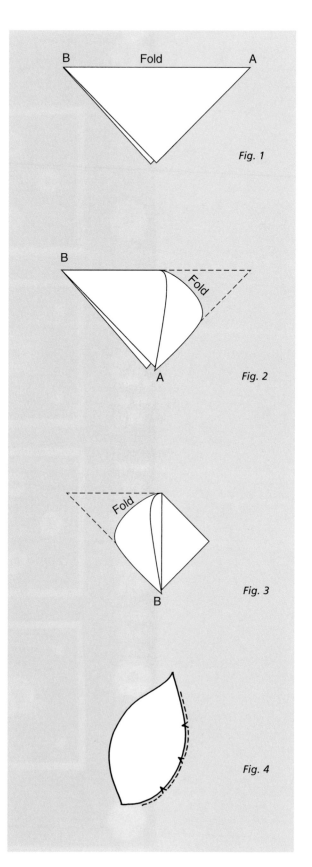

Fig. 1

Fig. 2

Fig. 3

Fig. 4

ASSEMBLING

STEP ONE

Cut the backing fabric in half, lengthwise, then rejoin the pieces to double the width. Press the seam open.

STEP TWO

Pin or tape the backing face down on the work surface. Centre the wadding on top. Place the quilt top on top of the wadding, facing upwards. Smooth out each layer as you put it down. Secure all the layers of the quilt sandwich, using the safety pins.

QUILTING

STEP ONE

Machine-quilt several times around the flower shapes in the blocks (Fig. 5). This is called echo-quilting and it makes the flowers stand out really well.

STEP TWO

Quilt a pattern in the sashing spaces and around the frames of the blocks, if you wish to. The more quilting you do on this quilt, the better it will look.

TO FINISH

STEP ONE

Trim the backing and the wadding to the size of the quilt top.

STEP TWO

Cut 9 cm (3¹/2 in) wide strips for the binding from the black fabric joining lengths, if necessary. Fold the binding over double, with the wrong sides together and the raw edges even. Sew the binding to the sides of the right side of the quilt with the raw edges even. When the binding is sewn to all four edges, turn the folded edge of the binding on to the back of the quilt. Slipstitch it in place, mitring the corners.

STEP THREE

Label your quilt.

YOU CAN USE STRAIGHT-CUT STEMS FOR THIS BLOCK

Fig. 5

USE BIAS-CUT STEMS FOR THIS BLOCK

BY LARRAINE SCOULER
This brilliantly colourful quilt gives appliqué a contemporary edge. Reminiscent of the traditional four-block quilts, it features designs that call to mind the court jesters of the middle ages.

Larraine has a revolutionary method for making appliqué quilts which avoids the difficulties of stop-start quilting around appliqué pieces – her quilts are pieced and quilted, then appliquéd. This way you don't have a multitude of loose thread ends to tie off – they are all at the sides of the quilt. This technique provides you with a firm and stable surface on which to appliqué and the quilted grid also acts as a guide for placement of the appliqué pieces.

This quilt is machine-pieced, machine-quilted and machine-appliquéd.

FINISHED SIZE
Quilt: 140 cm x 195 cm (52 in x 73 in)

FABRIC REQUIREMENTS
2 m (2¼ yd) of fabric for the background
1 m (1⅛ yd) each of two fabrics with good contrast for the chequerboard
20 cm (8 in) of fabric for the narrow stripe
30 cm (12 in) of fabric for the side border
30 cm (12 in) of fabric for the binding
150 cm x 205 cm (60 in x 83 in) of fabric for the backing
150 cm x 205 cm (60 in x 83 in) of wadding
50 cm (20 in) of green fabric for the leaves
Scraps of pink and yellow for the flower and dots

OTHER REQUIREMENTS
Sewing threads to match the background and the appliqué fabrics
750 (at least) 4 cm (1½ in) safety pins
Walking foot (optional)
Rotary cutter
Self-healing cutting mat
Quilter's ruler
Water-soluble fabric marker pen
Pencils
Template plastic
Lightweight cardboard, such as manilla folders
Masking tape
Spray starch

DETAIL OF THE CENTRE CHEQUERBOARD

CENTRE CHEQUERBOARD (A)
Note that the measurements include 7.5 mm (¼ in) seam allowances. Seams are generally pressed open to achieve a flatter quilt. The letters in the instructions refer to areas marked on the quilting diagram on page 105.

STEP ONE
From both chequerboard fabrics, cut eight 4 cm x 30 cm (1½ in x 12 in) strips. Sew the strips together, alternating the fabrics. Press.

STEP TWO
Straighten one edge and, using the rotary cutter, ruler and mat, cut the joined strips into seven units, each 4 cm (1½ in) wide.

STEP THREE
Piece a seven by seven square chequerboard, removing one square from each row to fit the pattern (Fig. 1). Press.

court jesters

court jesters

SIDE PANELS B

Cut two panels from the background fabric, each 19 cm x 46.75 cm (7¹/₂ in x 17¹/₄ in). Sew them to the sides of the centre chequerboard. Press.

CORNER CHEQUERBOARDS C

STEP ONE

From each chequerboard fabric, cut three 5.5 cm x 110 cm (2 in x 42 in) strips. Cut one 5.5 cm x 110 cm (2 in x 42 in) strip from the background fabric. Cut these into 5.5 cm (2 in) squares. Piece the four corner units, using the photograph as a guide, then using the ruler and rotary cutter, trim the background squares along the edge into triangles (Fig. 2). Press.

STEP TWO

Trim them to a triangle shape as shown, being careful to add seam allowance.

TOP AND BOTTOM PANELS D

STEP ONE

Cut two pieces of the background fabric, each 46.5 cm x 109.5 cm (17¹/₄ in x 41 in). Trim two 29 cm (10³/₄ in) triangles off each one as shown (Fig. 3).

STEP TWO

Position, pin and stitch the four pieced corner chequerboards to the top and bottom panels. Press.

STEP THREE

Sew the top and bottom panels to either side of centre panel. Press.

CHEQUERBOARD PANELS E AND F

STEP ONE

Cut 5.5 cm (2 in) wide strips across the width of both chequerboard fabrics. Sew a strip from each fabric together, lengthwise. Press. Cut them into 5.5 cm (2 in) wide units.

STEP TWO

Sew two panels of twenty-seven units for the sides and two panels of thirty-one units for the top and bottom (Fig. 4). Sew them to the quilt top.

TOP AND BOTTOM APPLIQUE PANEL G

Cut two panels from the background fabric, each measuring 21.5 cm x 125.5 cm (8 in x 47 in). Pin and stitch one to the top and one to the bottom of the pieced quilt top. Press.

SIDE BORDER H

STEP ONE

From the striped fabric, cut two 3 cm x 165.5 cm (1 in x 62 in) strips. From the border fabric, cut two 8 cm x 165.5 cm (3 in x 62 in) strips.

STEP TWO

Stitch one of each together, then sew them to the sides of the quilt top. Press.

TOP AND BOTTOM EXTENDED CHEQUERBOARD I

STEP ONE

Cut 5.5 cm (2 in) wide strips across the width of the fabric from each of the chequerboard fabrics. Stitch two of each together, lengthwise, alternating fabrics to form a four-strip band.

STEP TWO

Straighten one end of the band, then cut eighteen 5.5 cm (2 in) wide units and eighteen 13 cm (5 in) wide units. Continue making the four-strip bands, as required.

STEP THREE

Piece nine narrow units together end to end. Repeat for the wide units. Remove one square from one end to leave thirty-five squares, alternating the end colours on the wide and the narrow pieced rows. Stitch one wide and one narrow row together (Fig. 5). Press, then sew the quilt top.

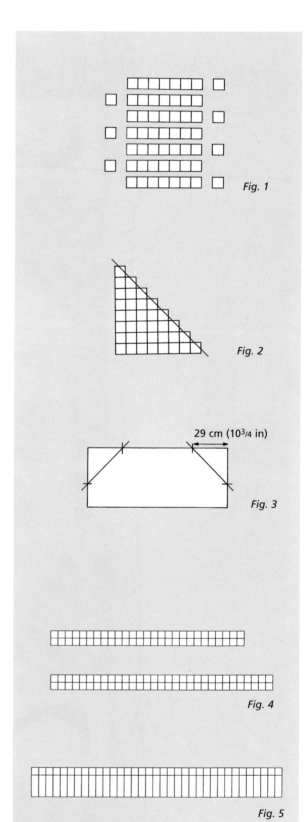

Fig. 1

Fig. 2

29 cm (10³/₄ in)

Fig. 3

Fig. 4

Fig. 5

QUILTING

STEP ONE

Mark a grid on the centre background panel and the top and bottom appliqué panels. This is really easy to do as the chequerboard already provides an accurately marked perimeter.

STEP TWO

The quilting pattern on the side border panels looks complicated but is easily marked, using the lower leaf appliqué shape. Cut a template of the shape from cardboard. Start in the centre and work out to the edges, mirror-imaging the design. Overlap the shapes slightly. Use the photograph as a guide.

STEP THREE

Cut and rejoin the backing fabric so it is slightly larger than the quilt top.

STEP FOUR

Pin or tape the backing, face down on the work surface. Centre the wadding on top, then the pieced top, face upwards, on top of that. Pin-baste every 10 cm (4 in) or so with the safety pins.

STEP FIVE

Quilt 'in-the-ditch' between the chequerboards and the main background. Stipple-quilt the chequerboards. Using a walking foot, if you have one, machine-quilt the straight grid lines. Take the thread ends through to the back of the quilt, knot them together, then thread them into a large-eyed needle and hide the ends in the wadding, for a neat, professional finish.

STEP SIX

Baste the edges of the quilt, through all thicknesses. Trim the backing and the wadding to the size of the quilt top.

BINDING

STEP ONE

Cut 6 cm (2¼ in) wide bias strips for the binding. Join them to achieve the required length. Fold the binding over double with the wrong sides facing. Press, taking care not to stretch or distort the binding.

STEP TWO

Pin the binding to the right side of the quilt, with all the raw edges matching and leaving a 10 cm (4 in) tail at the beginning and the end. Stitch, then join the ends of the binding. Turn the binding to the back of the quilt, mitring the corners. Stitch. For more information about binding, see page 152.

BACK TO FRONT APPLIQUE

See the pattern on Pull Out Pattern Sheet 2.

Note: There's no need to pre-mark the appliqué placement as the scaled drawing easily allows you to precisely position each shape on the background, using the quilted grid lines as a guide.

STEP ONE

From the templates provided, prepare one master plastic template for each shape, then trace and cut one cardboard shape for each area of the appliqué.

STEP TWO

Using the master template, cut a fabric piece for each shape, adding a 7.5 mm (¼ in) seam allowance. Baste the fabric over the edge of the cardboard. Lightly spray the seam allowance with starch and press, using the tip and edge of the iron. Leave them to cool.

STEP THREE

At the last moment, remove the basting and the cardboard. Position and pin the appliqué pieces in place. Straight-stitch machine-appliqué through all layers, using threads which blend with or contrast with the appliqué pieces. Tie ends off the ends of the threads as for the quilting. For more information about this method of straight-stitch appliqué, see page 85.

ALL THE APPLIQUE IS STITCHED WITH A STRAIGHT STITCH

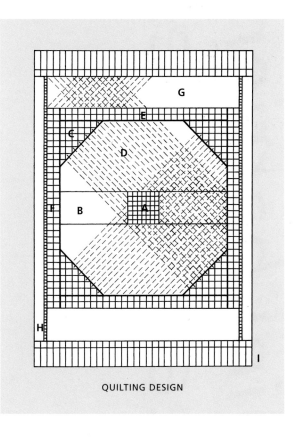

QUILTING DESIGN

mini barrier reef sampler

BY EILEEN CAMPBELL

This beautiful little quilt is actually a sampler, demonstrating a variety of stitching and appliqué techniques for which Eileen is famous.

The Barrier Reef theme provides the perfect canvas for displaying three-dimensional appliqué, free-standing appliqué and techniques using heat-vanishing muslin.

These techniques were explored previously in Eileen's wonderful quilt 'Marnie's Seagulls Visit the Reef' (previously published in *QuiltSkills*, J.B. Fairfax Press Pty Limited 1997). In this mini sampler, they have been distilled into a small wallhanging, which is not difficult to achieve.

For this quilt, collect fabrics which will provide a variety of textures in your chosen colours. Almost any fabric can be used with the Vliesofix technique described here, although some fabrics will need some protection from the direct heat of the iron.

Beads and rhinestones add an extra quality to the quilt. Flat-backed rhinestones can be attached with gemstone glue and give a wonderful sparkle and life to the eyes of the fish. Beads can also be used as eyes, or to highlight certain areas of the design.

This quilt is machine-appliquéd and machine-quilted.

FINISHED SIZE

Quilt: 52 cm x 65 cm (20$\frac{1}{2}$ in x 25$\frac{1}{2}$ in)

FABRIC REQUIREMENTS

Note: Fabric lengths allow for mitred corners.

38 cm x 51 cm (15 in x 20 in) of fabric for the central panel

3.5 cm x 200 cm (1$\frac{1}{4}$ in x 80 in) of fabric for the narrow border

6.5 cm x 230 cm (2$\frac{1}{2}$ in x 95 in) of fabric for the outer border

4 cm x 285 cm (1$\frac{1}{2}$ in x 112 in) of fabric for the binding

Small pieces of assorted fabrics suitable for appliqués with a sea theme (fish, seagull, palm tree trunk, dolphin, sand, coral)

18 cm x 40 cm (7 in x 16 in) of fabric for the rock platform

30 cm x 40 cm (12 in x 16 in) of fabric for the palm fronds

60 cm x 70 cm (24 in x 27 in) of fabric for the backing

60 cm x 70 cm (24 in x 27 in) of wadding

OTHER REQUIREMENTS

50 cm ($\frac{1}{2}$ yd) of Vliesofix

50 cm ($\frac{1}{2}$ yd) of iron-on stabiliser, such as Tear Away

50 cm ($\frac{1}{2}$ yd) of iron-on Vilene (medium/heavy weight)

25 cm ($\frac{1}{4}$ yd) of iron-on Pellon

One packet of heat-vanishing muslin, such as Heat-Away or Thermogaze

Machine-embroidery rayon threads in colours to match the appliqués and for the lacy corals

Bobbinfil or polycotton or polyester thread for the bobbin

Monofilament threads for quilting

Thick gold thread for couching

Machine-embroidery hoops (12–18 cm (5–7 in) spring hoop is good)

Sewing machine

Zigzag or open-toed embroidery foot

Darning foot

Metalfil or System N needle, size 75 or 80

Usual tracing and drawing supplies

Non-stick baking paper, such as GLAD Bake

Small amount (less than a handful) of dacron filling

Beads or flat-backed rhinestones

Gemstone glue

Usual sewing supplies

Masking tape

2.5 cm (1 in) safety pins

Tapestry needle

mini barrier reef sampler

TECHNIQUES
THE APPLIQUE METHOD

Vliesofix has been used for all the appliqués. Vliesofix is a double-sided fusible webbing with tracing paper on one side. It makes appliqué very simple, provided you remember one thing – your design must be drawn in reverse on the Vliesofix. To make it easy for this project, almost all the designs are provided already in reverse. All you need to do is trace them, as they are, onto the Vliesofix and your appliqués will come out as they are in the photograph. You will need to design the rock platform in step 3 and the palm leaves in step 6. These will then need to be reversed, when you trace them onto the Vliesofix.

Draw separately each part of a motif that will be on a different fabric. Where one piece adjoins another, allow a margin on the piece that will lie to the back to underlap the front piece.

Trace the reversed image onto the smooth, paper side of the Vliesofix. Cut out the traced motif, leaving a small margin all around. If you have many pieces to be cut from the same fabric, you can trace them in a block and handle them as one at this stage.

Using a medium-heat, dry iron, press the rough side of the Vliesofix onto the back of the appliqué fabric. Cut out the traced shapes exactly.

When you have cut out the appliqués, decide where you will place them on the background fabric, then peel the backing paper from the Vliesofix on each of the appliqués. Making sure that all the underlaps are in place and using a medium-heat, dry iron, press the pieces into position on the background.

Back your work with an iron-on stabiliser, extending it 2.5 cm (1 in) beyond all the appliqué pieces. Use iron-on Tear-Away, where the backing is to be removed, or iron-on Vilene, where it is to stay in place. Stitch the pieces into place on the background. Remove the stabiliser, if you are using Tear-Away.

THREADS

Best results are achieved using machine-embroidery rayon thread, number 40, especially for the satin stitching. Polycotton threads can also be used, but they will generally look more chunky and do not give the same sheen. For a heavier look, number 30 rayon embroidery thread can be used or, for some free-machine stitching which needs to stand out more, try Cotona 30.

There is a wide range of shiny metallic threads available. The easiest to use are the smooth-finish ones. These are excellent for highlights and for special effects.

Thicker threads which will not go through the machine can be couched down. Use a braiding foot and a zigzag stitch, about 1.5 mm wide by 1.5 mm long (less than 1/16 in long by less than 1/16 in wide).

In the bobbin, use a Bobbinfil or a fine polyester thread when appliquéing directly onto your background. If you are stitching the three-dimensional appliqués, it is best to use the same thread for the top and for the bobbin, as the colour will then be even on all the visible edges.

For all appliqué and machine-embroidery, it is best to use a Metalfil or System N needle, size 75 or 80. This needle has a bigger eye than usual and helps to stop the thread breaking.

STITCHING
SATIN STITCHING

For satin stitching, loosen the top tension by at least one stop. Your aim is to have the satin stitching pull underneath slightly, so that the top thread is seen on either side of the bobbin thread.

For most appliqués, the satin stitch width is between 1.5 mm and 2 mm (up to 1/16 in). Your stitches should rest mostly on the appliqué piece, coming over only slightly onto the background. Set the stitch length so that the stitching appears to be in a solid line, but not so close that the stitches bunch up. The complex mixtures of fabrics used can affect your machine settings, so practise sewing on some samples of the fused layers and stabilisers used in each particular item.

Begin and end the stitching with a few fastening stitches on one spot, or pull the top thread through and tie it off at the back.

The aim is to always sew at right angles to the edge of the appliqué piece you are stitching. Where you need to change the angle to go around a curve, stop with the needle in the wide part of the curve, lift the presser foot, turn your work slightly and do a few more stitches. Repeat this pivoting step as many times as you find it necessary to complete stitching the curve smoothly.

For points on the ends of leaves and so on, it is not

FREE-FORM PADDED APPLIQUE WAS USED FOR THE FISH

THE PALM FRONDS ARE STITCHED DOWN WITH FREE MACHINE-STITCHING

necessary to taper the stich. Continue to the top of the point. Leave the needle down and turn your work. Raise the needle and reposition the work, so that your first stitching in the other direction covers the previous couple of stitches. This will give you a blunt point and is very easy to do without affecting the good appearance.

FREE MACHINE-EMBROIDERY

To do this, you will need a darning foot and also be able to lower the feed dogs or cover them with a plate.

Set your machine for straight stitching with a stitch width and length set at 0. Tension should be normal, although you may have to lower it a little, depending on your stitching. Bring the bobbin thread up to the top of your work and hold both threads as you take the first few stitches. After that you can stitch in any direction. Some appliqués are best stitched using this technique – for example, the palm tree and the highlight on the sand. Attach the appliqué pieces using the Vliesofix technique, but instead of satin stitching, hold the pieces down with free machine-stitching. You might use a combination of stitches: satin stitch for the trunk and free machine-stitching for the leaves. Free machine-stitching is also used to embellish appliqués, defining the veins in leaves and the fish fins.

FREE MACHINE-STITCHING USING HEAT-VANISHING MUSLIN

This technique was used for some corals and the feather stars on the quilt. Heat-vanishing muslin (sold as Heat-Away or Thermogaze) can be put into a hoop and embroidered on. Ironing will turn it into a brown powder that can be brushed away, leaving the embroidery intact. Heat-vanishing muslin is best stored in a cool dark place.

When embroidering on heat-vanishing muslin, use the same thread on top and in the bobbin. Make sure that all your embroidery lines are connected so that your piece will not fall apart when the supporting heat-vanishing muslin is removed. You can draw on it easily with a pencil if you need guidelines.

FREE-FORM PADDED APPLIQUE

This technique was used for the tropical fish, seagull and coral. Follow the steps for the appliqué method up to the cutting out of the pieces. Cut a piece of backing fabric large enough to hold all the appliqués (flowers, leaves, etc) plus 1 cm (3/8 in) all around. If the backs of your finished appliqués are likely to show, then choose an appropriate fabric for the backs. Cut a piece of iron-on Vilene the same size as the backing fabric. Fuse the iron-on Vilene to the back of the backing fabric. Cut a piece of iron-on Pellon to the same size as the backing fabric. If

iron-on Pellon is not available, use ordinary Pellon and Vliesofix. Cut a piece of Vliesofix the same size as the Pellon and fuse them together. Carefully peel away the tracing paper from the Vliesofix and you now have Pellon which you can fuse to the backing. Use GLAD Bake between the Pellon and the iron.

Peel the tracing paper from the appliqué pieces and fuse them to the backing, again using GLAD Bake underneath the iron. Satin stitch, embellish, cut out and finish the pieces. Machine- or hand-embroidery can be done at this stage; for example, the fish fins. Cut out the appliqués. It is easiest to use a small pair of sharp scissors and angle them underneath your work as you cut, being very careful not to cut the satin stitch threads. If you do cut a thread (as always happens), use a fray stopper or a drop of clear craft glue on the end of a toothpick to prevent the stitch from unravelling.

If the cut edges of the iron-on Vilene are too visible, colour them carefully with a fabric marker pen. If you prefer a less padded effect, use one or two layers of iron-on Vilene instead of the one layer of iron-on Vilene and one layer of Pellon as described above.

TO ATTACH THE PIECES

In this project, the padded appliqué pieces were attached to the main background after it was quilted.

The coral was attached at its base into a seam or with monofilament thread within a panel. Using free-machining, catch the coral at various points, so that the pieces will not droop, but in such a way that they will still look free and give a three-dimensional appearance. Some branches of coral, especially near the bottom of a piece, can be given a quilted outline in monofilament thread as they are attached, to accentuate them more.

Birds and fish can be attached with monofilament thread, using free machine-stitching very close to the satin stitching around the body. Leave the fish fins free for a more realistic look.

As well as the padding that the Pellon provides, the bodies of the seagull or fish can be further padded as they are attached. To do this, stitch halfway around the creature's body and, using a small amount of polyester filling, stuff the body before completing the stitching. A satay stick or something similar, is very useful for hard-to-reach corners and for evening-out the filling.

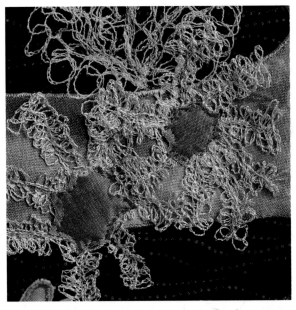

THE CORAL WAS CREATED USING HEAT-VANISHING MUSLIN

EILEEN HAS FINISHED HER QUILT WITH A FABULOUS LABEL

APPLIQUE

See the patterns on pages 112–115.

STEP ONE

For the sand and palm tree trunks, using the Vliesofix appliqué technique, cut out the sand, sand highlight and palm tree trunks. Fuse them all into place on the background with the bottom edge of the sand about 29 cm (11½ in) from the top left of the centre panel. Back them with iron-on stabiliser and satin stitch around the sand and palm tree trunks. Free machine-stitch over the sand highlight.

STEP TWO

Using the three-dimensional appliqué technique, construct the five pieces of padded coral.

STEP THREE

Design and stitch the rock platform. The top of this begins approximately 6.5 cm (2½ in) up from the bottom left side of the centre panel and weaves its way to approximately 18 cm (7 in) up on the right side of the panel. For a guide see the quilt photograph. Remember to trace the rock platform in reverse on the Vliesofix, then fuse it to the back of the rock platform fabric. Cut it out, but before fusing it in place, tuck the bottoms of two padded coral pieces (1 and 2) underneath one section, pinning them in place. Back this section with iron-on stabiliser, then satin stitch the rock platform in place, stitching over the ends of the coral.

STEP FOUR

Pin the narrow border to the top and bottom, pinning the two padded coral pieces (3 and 4) in the bottom seam. Stitch, then attach the side borders, mitring the corners.

STEP FIVE

Attach the wide border, mitring the corners.

STEP SIX

For the palm fronds, draw long frond shapes with rounded ends, some large, some smaller, curving to the left and right. You will need ten to twelve of them. Remember to trace them in reverse on the Vliesofix. Having cut the Vliesofix-backed fronds in the basic shapes, mark a central vein and cut curved V-shapes almost up to this line all the way around the edge. Arrange the fronds on the tree trunks, overlapping a little in places. Back them with stabiliser and free machine-stitch them in place, making sure each leaf spike on the frond has at least one line of stitching to hold it in place.

STEP SEVEN

For the dolphin and lower sand area, using the Vliesofix appliqué method and satin stitching, fix the dolphin in place on the left side, just above the rock platform. Stitch the sand on the right side of the lower border. Free machine-stitch the sand highlight in place.

STEP EIGHT

Remove as much stabiliser as possible from the back of the work. Press the quilt top and the backing well.

QUILTING
STEP ONE

Place the backing fabric face down. Tape the corners so they are taut but not stretched. Centre the wadding on top and tape it in place as well. Place the quilt top on top of that, face upwards. There should be a little extra wadding and backing showing all round. Tape down the corners of the quilt top.

STEP TWO

Using 2.5 cm (1 in) safety pins, pin along the edge of one long side. Next pin the opposite long side and, lastly, the two short sides. Now pin into the centre, beginning at the sides and working in. The pins should be about 8–10 cm (3–4 in) apart. Try not to pin on the appliqué pieces. Take the pins out again as you quilt.

STEP THREE

Quilt 'in-the-ditch' on both sides of the narrow border. Use free machine-stitching to outline the sand, rock platform, dolphin and palm tree trunks. The background can be quilted with wavy lines to represent the sea. Lift the pieces of coral and quilt under them also.

THREE-DIMENSIONAL PIECES
STEP ONE

For the lilac feather star, gorgonian coral and organ pipe coral, use free machine-stitching with heat-vanishing muslin. Make the feather star in two pieces. Place the one with feet on top, when stitching it in place under the dolphin. Draw a guide for the gorgonian coral on heat-vanishing muslin, then join the 'branches' with lacy lines, making sure all are connected. Organ pipe coral has eight arms. Machine-embroider them in a circle, approximately 6.5 cm (2½ in) in diameter, as a whole unit. Cut a Vliesofix-backed eight-sided star shape from fabric and fuse it over the centre of the completed organ pipe coral. Pin it in place until you have begun stitching.

STEP TWO

For the padded fish and seagull, use free-form padded appliqué. The blue lines on the large fish fins are made with satin stitching.

TO FINISH

STEP ONE

Attach the binding, mitring the seams, adding the last piece of padded coral (5) in the seam. Turn the binding to the back and slipstitch it in place. See page 152 for how to bind a quilt.

STEP TWO

Couch gold thread to outline the narrow border. Use a braiding foot to hold the gold thread and zigzag over it using monofilament thread on top and a thread to match the backing in the bobbin. The ends of the gold thread can be threaded on a tapestry needle and buried in the wadding. Couch the thread between the palm fronds, not over them.

STEP THREE

Stitch all the embroidered pieces and padded appliqués in place.

STEP FOUR

For the eyes and highlights (bubble trails behind the fish), stitch beads in place or use flat-backed rhinestones and gemstone glue.

STEP FIVE

Label your quilt. Stitch a hanging sleeve on the back and your 'Mini Barrier Reef Sampler' is ready to hang. For more information on how to make and attach a hanging sleeve, see page 153.

THE FEATHER STARS ARE MADE IN TWO SECTIONS USING HEAT-VANISHING MUSLIN

'MARNIE'S SEAGULLS VISIT THE REEF'
186 CM X 222 CM (73 IN X 83 IN)

COMPLETE ALL THE SATIN STITCHING, BEFORE CUTTING OUT THE CORAL

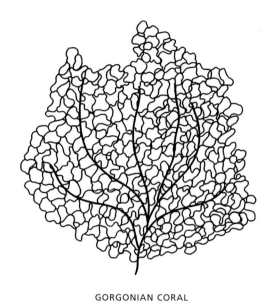

GORGONIAN CORAL

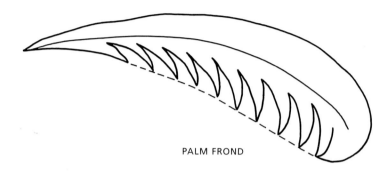

PALM FROND

CORAL 4

CORAL 2

CORAL 5

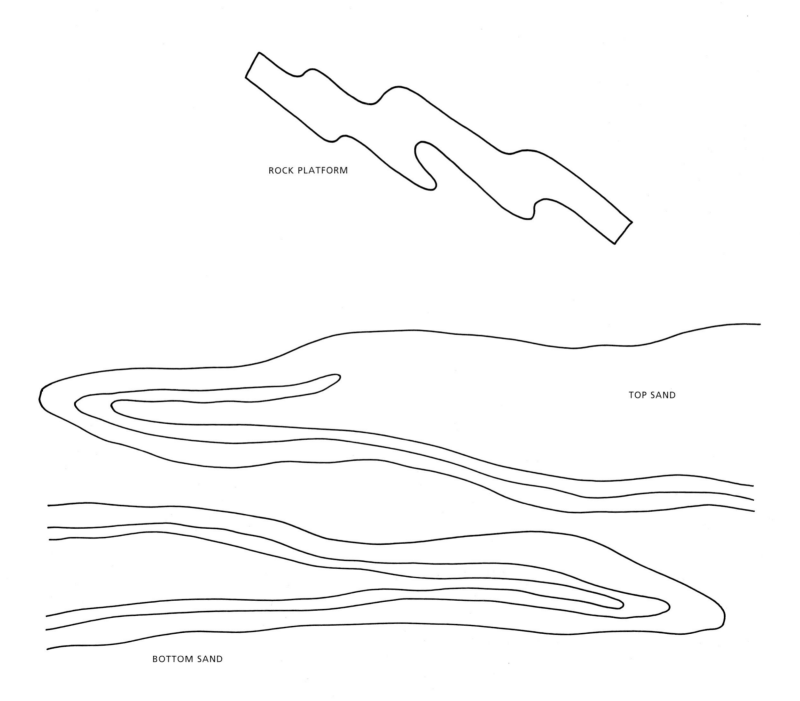

ROCK PLATFORM

TOP SAND

BOTTOM SAND

DOLPHIN

ORGAN PIPE CORAL

SILVERGULL

CORAL 3

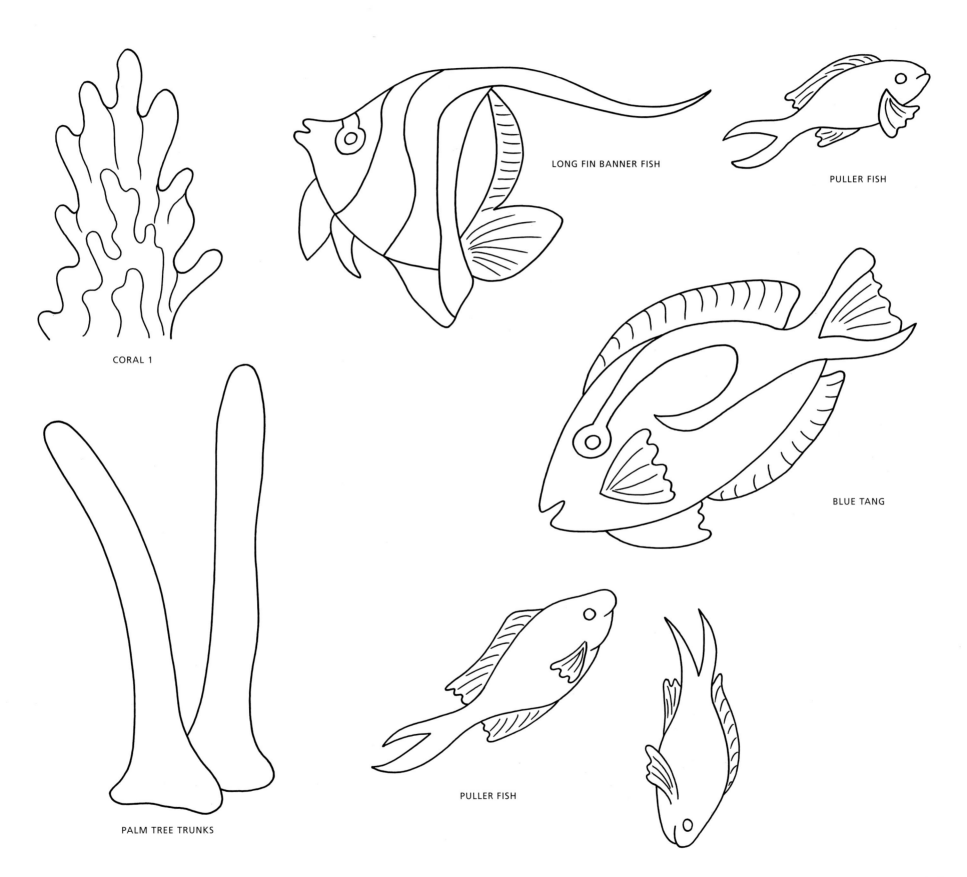

CORAL 1

LONG FIN BANNER FISH

PULLER FISH

BLUE TANG

PALM TREE TRUNKS

PULLER FISH

BY WENDY SMITH

This wonderful quilt won the Viewers' Choice Award at a NSW Quilter's Guild Exhibition. The design is very elegant throughout and allows the appliqué to be the main feature.

Wendy used a pale pink self-patterned background and a variety of scrap fabrics in pinks and greens for the roses and leaves. The extensive and complex quilting is a feature of Wendy's quilt, but you could use a simple grid pattern, if you prefer.

When the quilting was completed, Wendy stuffed certain areas to create a raised effect.

This quilt is hand-appliquéd and hand-quilted.

FINISHED SIZE

Quilt: 198 cm (78 in) square

FABRIC REQUIREMENTS

5 m (5 1/2 yd) of pale pink fabric for the background
50 cm (20 in) scraps of pink and green fabrics for the appliqué
1 m (1 1/8 yd) of blue/grey fabric for the scallops
4 m (4 1/2 yd) of fabric for the backing
80 cm (32 in) of fabric for the binding
205 cm (81 in) square of wadding

OTHER REQUIREMENTS

Pencil
Freezer paper
Template plastic
Scalpel
Self-healing cutting mat
Fineline permanent marker pen
Water-soluble fabric marker pen
Hand-sewing needles
Matching sewing threads
Quilting threads
4 cm (1 1/2 in) safety pins
Scissors
Glass-headed pins
Quilter's hoop
Masking tape
3-ply white cording
Tapestry needle

CUTTING

See the appliqué templates and quilting designs on Pull Out Pattern Sheet 1. The templates do not include seam allowances. Add 7.5 mm (1/4 in) seam allowances to all the templates when cutting them out of fabric. The cut strips and squares include 7.5 mm (1/4 in) seam allowances and extra length for mitring.

STEP ONE

Using the pencil, trace the templates for the roses and leaves from the pattern sheet onto the freezer paper – do not add seam allowances. Cut them out exactly on the pencil lines.

STEP TWO

Iron the freezer paper pieces onto the back of the fabrics you have selected for the roses and leaves. Make sure you have a variety of shades from light to dark for each rose. Cut the shapes out of the fabric, adding 7.5 mm (1/4 in) seam allowances all around.

STEP THREE

Note: The following measurements include 7.5 mm (1/4 in) seam allowances.

From the background fabric, cut the following pieces:
• four strips, 31.5 cm x 200 cm (12 1/2 in x 79 in) for the appliqué border;
• four strips, 4.5 cm x 140 cm (1 3/4 in x 55 1/8 in) for the inner scallops; four strips 6.5 cm x 210 cm (2 1/2 in x 82 1/2 in) for the outer scallops;
• five 46 cm (18 in) squares (A);
• one 48 cm (18 3/4 in) square, cut into quarters, diagonally, to yield four quarter-square triangles (B); and
• two 47 cm (18 3/8 in) squares, cut in half, diagonally, to yield four half-square triangles (C).

STEP FOUR

From the green fabric, cut 3 cm (1 1/4 in) wide bias strips for the stems. See page 152 for how to cut continuous bias strips. Press the bias strips over double with the wrong sides together.

everything's coming up roses

everything's coming up roses

APPLIQUE

STEP ONE

Arrange a circle of roses, leaves and stems on a background square, using the photograph as a guide. You can trace the design on to the background fabric with the fabric marker pen or the pencil, if you prefer. Pin the pieces in place, overlapping them where necessary.

STEP TWO

Using a small running stitch, sew the bias strips for the stems in place, stitching close to the raw edge of the strip (Fig. 1). Press the folded edge of the strip over to cover the raw edge, then appliqué it in place with a small running stitch which goes through the background fabric and catches only a few small threads in the piece being appliquéd (Fig. 2).

STEP THREE

Hand-appliqué the roses and leaves in the same way, using the shank of the needle to turn under the seam allowance as you go. You may need to trim the seam allowance a little, if you find it too cumbersome. Make four blocks with the circle of appliqué and one block with a flower spray in each corner for the centre of the quilt.

PIECING

When all the appliqué on the blocks is completed, join the squares and triangles into three strips as shown, in the assembly diagram, then join the three strips together to complete the quilt top.

INNER SCALLOPED BORDER

STEP ONE

Measure the length of the quilt top, measuring through the centre. Cut two 3 cm (1$^1/_4$ in) wide borders from the background fabric to this length. Measure the width of the quilt top, measuring through the centre and cut two 3 cm (1$^1/_4$ in) wide borders from the background fabric to this length.

STEP TWO

From the fabric for the scallops, cut 144 scallops, using template A and eight corner scallops, using template B. Add seam allowances to these pieces as you cut them out. Mark the mitres at the ends of the inner border pieces. Hand-appliqué the A pieces around the inner border pieces, using the same method as for the roses, taking care to stop the scallops just short of the markings for the mitres.

STEP THREE

Sew on the inner borders, mitring the corners.

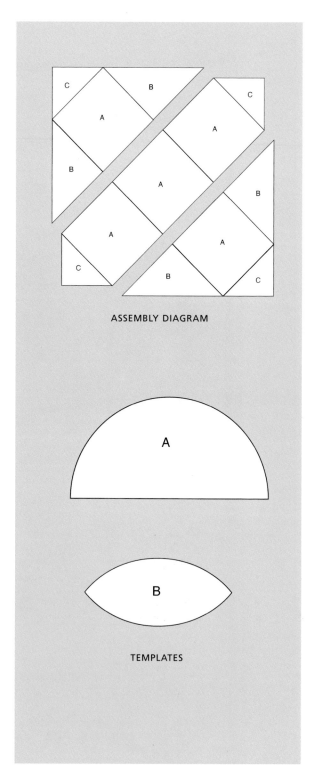

ASSEMBLY DIAGRAM

TEMPLATES

QUILT THE BACKGROUND WITH A CLOSE GRID

APPLIQUE BORDER

Measure, cut and sew the border in the same way as for the inner border, mitring the corners. Hand-appliqué the garlands of roses and leaves in the same way as for the quilt blocks.

OUTER SCALLOPED BORDER

STEP ONE

Measure and cut the 5 cm (2 in) wide outer border as for the inner border. Cut out and appliqué 140 scallops (as for the inner border), then sew on the outer border, mitring the corners.

STEP TWO

Appliqué the eight pieces cut using template B onto the corners of the scalloped borders.

ASSEMBLING

STEP ONE

Trace the quilting designs from the pattern sheet onto the template plastic. Make stencils for the quilting by cutting out the design with a scalpel. Transfer the designs to the quilt top, using the fabric marker pen or pencil.

STEP TWO

Cut the backing fabric in half, then rejoin the pieces to double the width.

STEP THREE

Pin or tape the backing fabric face down on the work surface. Centre the wadding on top. Place the completed quilt top on top of that, facing upwards. Smooth out any wrinkles as you place each layer. Secure the layers of the quilt sandwich with the safety pins. You can baste all the layers together, if you prefer.

QUILTING

Hand-quilt the entire quilt, including the borders.

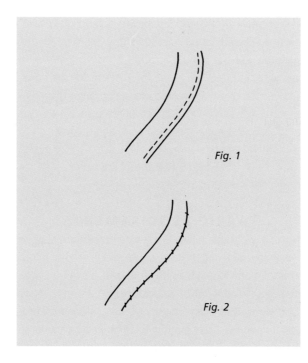

Fig. 1

Fig. 2

TO FINISH

STEP ONE

Trim the wadding and the backing to the size of the quilt top.

STEP TWO

Cut strips of 10 cm (4 in) wide fabric for the binding. Join strips as necessary to achieve the lengths required. Fold the binding over double with the wrong sides together and the raw edges even. Sew the binding to the four sides of the quilt with the raw edges even. Turn the folded edge of the binding over to the wrong side of the quilt, then slipstitch it in place, mitring the corners.

STEP THREE

This part takes a lot of courage! When her quilt was completely finished and bound, Wendy decided which parts of the design she wanted to stuff to make them stand out in the quilt. She then turned the quilt over and cut tiny slits in the backing through which she poked the white cording, using the tapestry needle. When all the stuffing was completed, she sewed up the slits with tiny, nearly invisible stitches.

STEP FOUR

Label your quilt.

THE CENTRE MEDALLION

AREAS OF QUILTING HAVE BEEN STUFFED

1920s floral appliqué

This delightful quilt comes from the collection of Annette Gero, a prominent Australian quilt historian and collector. It dates from the 1920s and was made from one of the kits which were popular at the time. The kit provided the maker with a top on which all the appliqué and quilting patterns were marked with blue, indelible ink.

The original kits also included the pre-cut appliqué pieces, each numbered to correspond with a marking on the quilt top. For this project, a variety of flower patterns in various sizes are given, as are the patterns for the bows. Choose the ones you wish to use and arrange them in a graceful oval shape in the centre of the quilt.

This quilt is hand-appliquéd and hand-quilted.

FINISHED SIZE

Quilt: 197 cm x 222 cm (77 3/4 in x 87 1/2 in)

FABRIC REQUIREMENTS

Note: It is possible to buy extra-wide homespun fabric to make the quilt top from a single piece. If this is not available, purchase 4.8 m (5 yd) of 112 cm (44 in) wide homespun. Cut it in half to produce two 2.4 m (2 1/2 yd) long pieces. Cut one of these pieces in half, lengthwise, and join one of these lengths to either side of the large piece of fabric. This way you will have sufficient length and the joining seam will run along the sides of the quilt.

Sufficient cream homespun fabric

Scraps of pastel fabrics for the appliqué

207 cm x 232 cm (81 3/4 in x 91 1/2 in) of thin wadding

207 cm x 232 cm (81 3/4 in x 91 1/2 in) of fabric for the backing

50 cm (20 in) of fabric for the binding

OTHER REQUIREMENTS

Tracing paper
Template plastic
Scalpel
Self-healing cutting mat
Black fineline marker pen
Thin cardboard
Pencil
Stranded cotton for the embroidery
Sewing thread to match the appliqués
Quilting thread
Quilting needles
Quilter's hoop
Sewing needles
Masking tape
Usual sewing supplies

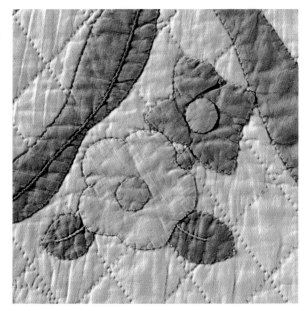

POSITION THE FLOWERS IN A PLEASING ARRANGEMENT

APPLIQUE

See the appliqué patterns and the quilting patterns on Pull Out Pattern Sheet 3.

STEP ONE

Trace the flowers, bows and leaves onto the tracing paper. Transfer the pattern onto the cardboard and cut it out exactly on the pencil line to make the templates. Make at least one template for each flower in each size.

STEP TWO

Following the picture opposite and the detail on page 123, determine how many of each flower and leaf are required or use your own design. Place the template on the right side of the appliqué fabric and draw around it with the pencil. Cut them out with a very small seam allowance, approximately 3 mm (1/8 in). Do this for all the appliqué pieces, remembering to mirror-reverse the ribbon swag.

STEP THREE

From the fabric for the stems, cut bias strips 20 mm (3/4 in) wide. Fold in a scant 7.5 mm (1/4 in) on both sides. These days, there are various devices to help you cut and sew lengths of bias accurately, such as bias folders, or you can make a cardboard template for the stems that has a finished width of 7.5 mm (1/4 in). If you are using the

1920s floral appliqué

template, cut out the fabric, centre the template on the wrong side and press the seam allowance in over the template. Press well, then remove the cardboard. Prepare the appropriate number of stems for the bouquet and for the garland, joining strips if necessary. See page 85 for more information about stems and vines.

STEP FOUR

On the quilt top, lightly mark with pencil the outline of the oval shape for the garland. It measures approximately 103 cm x 133 cm (40 in x 52 in). You can also mark the position of the flowers, if you wish. It is a good idea to lay out your flowers at this stage to check that you are happy with the arrangement. Make a quick sketch of your final layout, with the flowers identified by number.

STEP FIVE

Baste or pin the vine into position. Baste or pin on the leaves, tucking the ends under the vine. Using a green thread to match the vine and leaves, appliqué them into place, turning the seam allowance under with the shank of the needle as you go and using tiny slipstitches. It is best to work on a section at a time.

STEP SIX

Appliqué the ribbon swag and the flowers into position on the vine, in the same way as before. Appliqué the flower centres. You may find this easier to do, if you clip into the seam allowance.

You may prefer to prepare the flower centres by basting them over cardboard to ensure perfect circles. Cut the appropriate circles from the cardboard. Place the cardboard circle on the wrong side of the fabric and draw around it. Cut the fabric out with a 7.5 mm (1/4 in) seam allowance. Gather the edge of the circle with small running stitches. Pull up the gathering, drawing the seam allowance over the cardboard. Press well. Remove the cardboard carefully.

STEP SEVEN

Mark, pin and appliqué the central bouquet in the same way, tucking the ends of the stems under the flower heads at one end and under the knot of the bow at the other end. Add the bow last of all.

STEP EIGHT

Using two strands of cotton, embroider the vein lines on the leaves and the petal lines on the lilies and bluebells in stem stitch. The calyx is worked in yellow in satin stitch.

QUILTING

See the quilting patterns on Pull Out Pattern Sheet 3. You can trace and make stencils of these or you can use commercial quilting stencils, if you prefer.

STEP ONE

Trace the quilting patterns onto the template plastic. Cut out the pattern using the scalpel. For more information on how to cut quilting stencils, see page 10. Mark the quilting patterns on the quilt top. There is an overall diagonal grid pattern of lines 3.5 cm (1³/8 in) apart, a pattern of lilies and leaves inside and at opposite ends of the oval garland, a garland of bows around the outside of the oval and an intricate corner pattern of lilies and leaves. You may choose to include only one or two of these, or all of them.

STEP TWO

Pin or tape the backing fabric face down on the work surface. Centre the wadding on top. Place the quilt top on top of the wadding, face up. Smooth out all the wrinkles. Pin or baste the layers together and secure the quilt in the hoop, ready for quilting.

STEP THREE

Using the cream quilting thread and quilting needle, quilt your chosen patterns.

HINT

For reasons of space, only elements of the intricate quilting patterns are given on the pattern sheet. Many commercial quilting stencils will work beautifully on this quilt.

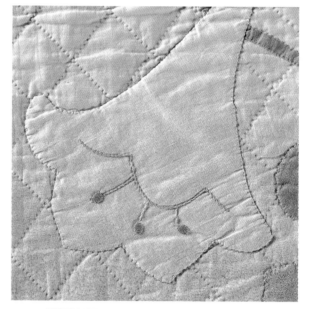

EMBELLISH THE APPLIQUE WITH EMBROIDERY

THE CORNER QUILTING PATTERN

TO FINISH

See the scallop pattern on Pull Out Pattern Sheet 3.

STEP ONE

Make a cardboard template of the scallop. Using the pencil, draw in the scalloped edge on the quilt. You may need to adjust the shape slightly to make it fit perfectly at the corners. Make a separate cardboard template for the corner scallops. Trim the quilt top, wadding and backing to the scallop shape.

STEP TWO

Cut the fabric for the binding into 4 cm (1^1/$_2$ in) wide bias strips. If you have not used the continuous binding method to cut the strips, join them now. (See page 152 for how to cut continuous bias binding.) Fold the binding over double, with the wrong sides facing. Press. Pin the binding to the quilt front with all the raw edges matching and shaping the binding around the curves. You can carefully use the iron to encourage the binding to curve gently. Stitch in a 7.5 mm (1/4 in) seam. Turn the binding to the back of the quilt and slipstitch it in place, by hand. If you have little tucks at the inner corners of the scallops and can't smooth them with the iron, you could catch them with a couple of tiny stitches.

STEP THREE

Label your quilt.

special techniques

Quiltmaking has become an art with many facets, which all add to the richness and breadth of the work. In this section, some of these interesting avenues are explored, including broderie perse, miniatures, shadow trapunto and more.

crazy patchwork pincushion

BY VIRGINIA ENRIGHT
Crazy patchwork is a delightful, traditional form of quilting with a unique richness. This little pincushion offers an opportunity to explore this lovely facet of patchwork and create an item of timeless appeal.

'If a lady wants to produce a startling effect in crazy patchwork, the first thing she has to do is to collect a quantity of scraps of silk, satin, brocade and velvet in the most heterogeneous colours. Then she has to cut them in all manners of shapes, carefully avoiding all geometric regularity ... The various patches are then to be embroidered with a variety of devices, such as the wildest imagination may suggest ... All sorts of silks and threads, so long as they are bright-coloured and shining, ought to be used for the embroidery, and gold or silver tinsel and cords lavishly employed for edging, dotting and outlining.'

This quotation from the widely read English magazine, *The Queen*, of July 1884, may well have encouraged the increasing popularity of crazy patchwork in the late nineteenth century. The late Victorian taste was for rooms crowded with ornate furniture, pattern on pattern in wallpaper, upholstery and drapery. Crazy patchwork with its rich fabrics and extravagant embellishments fitted perfectly into this style. In addition, having free time for fine needlework signalled a lady's social standing; crazy patchwork gave her an opportunity to show off her skills.

Crazy patchwork was used to create a wide range of items, personal and domestic. However, because of the types of fabrics used and the intricate embroidery, these were mainly for display. A crazy patchwork quilt was usually the best in the house and only brought out on special occasions.

Often women would use fabric or ribbons that held special meaning, such as a piece from a wedding dress or the ribbon from a bouquet. Names and meaningful dates were often embroidered on these pieces, as were messages, such as 'Good Luck'.

This pincushion is hand-pieced.

FINISHED SIZE

11 cm (4½ in) square

FABRIC REQUIREMENTS

12 cm (4¾ in) square of cream calico for the foundation
Scraps of various fabrics (Virginia used moiré taffeta from a sample card, but any luxurious fabrics will do)
12 cm (4¾ in) square of fabric for the backing

OTHER REQUIREMENTS

Stranded cotton
Metallic threads
Beads, buttons, trinkets etc
60 cm (24 in) of fine black cord
Polyester fibrefill
Spray starch
Usual sewing supplies

CUTTING

Note: This method of crazy patchwork works best for small pieces, such as pincushions, individual blocks and evening purses.

STEP ONE

Cut the fabrics into randomly shaped, four-sided patches. For this small piece it is a good idea to keep the sides straight, rather than curved. Spraying the back of the fabric pieces with starch and pressing them will make them easier to handle, especially if they are soft or flimsy.

STEP TWO

Choose the scrap which will go in the centre and trim it to make it a five-sided patch (Fig. 1).

PIECING

STEP ONE

Pin the centre patch to the centre of the foundation square. Pin the next patch onto one edge of the first patch, with the right sides together. Stitch along the matched edge in a 7.5 mm (1/4 in) seam, stitching through both patches and the foundation fabric (Fig. 2). Turn the second piece back, so the right side is up. Press or finger-press the seam.

STEP TWO

Working along another side of the first piece, attach another piece in the same way as before (Fig. 3). Trim away any excess fabric behind the patch. Continue attaching patches in this way (Fig. 4). When the first 'round' is completed, continue with another round until the entire foundation square is covered. If you are going to use lace, sew it onto the patch, before the patch is sewn onto the foundation square. When attaching patches it is better to aim for T intersections, rather than Xs (Fig. 5).

EMBROIDERY

STEP ONE

Trim the edges of the patches straight and even with the edges of the foundation. Press the whole piece well.

STEP TWO

Embellish the seams with various embroidery stitches, using two strands of embroidery cotton or metallic threads. Some suitable stitches are blanket stitch, fly stitch, chain stitch and herringbone stitch. This embroidery can be as ornate as you wish it to be.

STEP THREE

Sew on any beads, buttons or trinkets.

ASSEMBLING

STEP ONE

With the right sides facing, pin the crazy patchwork piece to the backing piece. Stitch in a 7.5 mm (1/4 in) seam, leaving an opening for turning and filling. Trim the corners and turn through, taking care that the corners are pushed out neatly. Fill the pincushion firmly with the polyester fibrefill, taking care to push the filling right into the corners. Close the opening by hand.

STEP TWO

Starting at one corner, slipstitch the black cord around the edge of the pincushion, over the seam. Form the cord into a loop at each corner and hold the loop in place with a few tiny stitches. Finish neatly where the ends of the cord meet. One way to do this is to carefully unpick a few stitches of the seam, tuck the ends inside and close the opening up again.

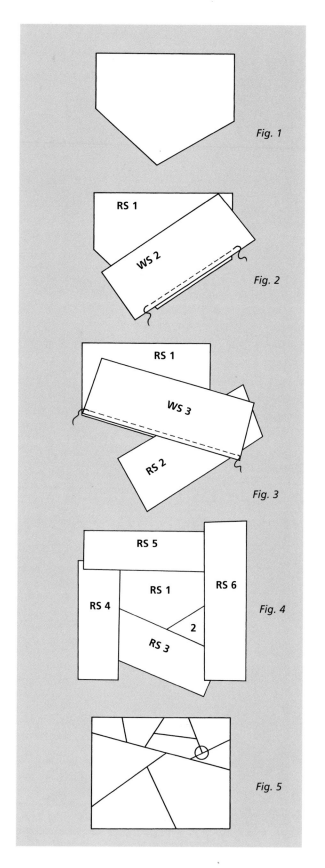

Fig. 1

Fig. 2

Fig. 3

Fig. 4

Fig. 5

PIN THE FIRST PATCH IN PLACE

SEW ANY LACE OR TRIMS IN PLACE

EMBELLISH WITH EMBROIDERY STITCHES

SEW THE BRAID ON BY HAND

BY VIRGINIA ENRIGHT

A miniature quilt which captures the colour and feel of a summer's day makes a perfect wallhanging.

Miniature quilts originally made for cribs and dolls' beds have a unique charm. Often made by mothers for their little girls or stitched by the children themselves, these tiny patches of history capture the past in a very special way. Unfortunately they were often made without the same attention and care that was put into a full-sized quilt, and the fabrics used were generally less durable, so few of these delightful pieces remain.

Today, miniature quilts are again very popular. Less likely to be found on a doll's bed, they are often displayed on walls, as this example is. Many quiltmakers are challenged by the tiny scale of these quilts and enjoy the requirement of meticulous care.

The same considerations of design apply to miniature quilts as to their larger cousins, especially as regards fabric. Use one hundred per cent cotton fabrics, and wash and press them before you begin. The tiny scale means that easy-to-work-with fabrics are crucial to success. Choose prints whose scale works comfortably with the scale of the blocks. Larger, splashy prints should be reserved for the borders.

Remember, slight irregularities which can be absorbed in a large block will be glaringly obvious in a miniature. Accuracy in both cutting and piecing is crucial. For this reason, many makers of miniature quilts prefer to work on a foundation, which ensures absolute accuracy. Check all the points as you work, to make sure they meet.
The quick and accurate piecing method used for this quilt is suitable only for machine-piecing. Some fabric is wasted using this method, but only a very small amount, and the method is very accurate.

This quilt is machine-pieced and machine-quilted.

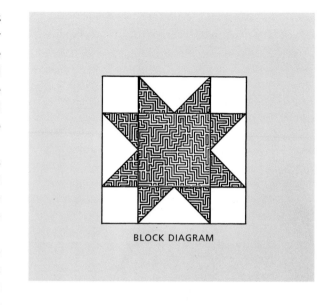

BLOCK DIAGRAM

FINISHED SIZE
Quilt: 30 cm (10½ in) square
Block size: 6 cm (2 in) square
Total number of blocks: nine

FABRIC REQUIREMENTS
20 cm (8 in) each of yellow fabric and blue fabric
20 cm (8 in) of fabric for the border
30 cm (12 in) of cream fabric for the background
30 cm (12 in) square of fabric for the backing
30 cm (12 in) square of thin wadding

OTHER REQUIREMENTS
Rotary cutter
Self-healing cutting mat
Quilter's ruler
Spray starch
Usual sewing supplies
4 cm (1½ in) safety pins

miniature star quilt

CUTTING

STEP ONE

Note: A seam allowance of 7.5 mm (^{1}/4 in) has been included in all the measurements.

Cut the cream, yellow and blue fabrics into 3.5 cm x 33 cm (1^1/2 in x 13 in) strips, using the rotary cutter, quilter's ruler and mat.

STEP TWO

Cut four yellow and five blue 4.5 cm (1^1/2 in) centre squares for the blocks.

STEP THREE

Cut thirty-six 3 cm (1 in) squares of background fabric.

STEP FOUR

Using the rotary cutter, quilter's ruler and mat, cut the border fabric into 7 cm (2^1/2 in) wide strips.

PIECING

Note: Press all the pieces using the spray starch. This will make the small pieces of fabric much easier to handle.

STEP ONE

Machine-sew each blue strip to a background strip and each yellow strip to a background strip, using a small stitch and keeping an accurate 7.5 mm (^{1}/4 in) seam allowance. Press the seam allowance towards the darker fabric, making sure that the seam is absolutely flat and that there are no tucks on the seam line.

STEP TWO

Using the rotary cutter and ruler, cut 3 cm (1 in) squares from the strips, as shown. To do this, place the diagonal of the ruler along the seam line and cut. Each square will be half yellow or blue and half cream. You can, of course, make a template of the square, draw around it and cut out the squares using scissors, if you prefer.

STEP THREE

Join two pieced squares (Fig. 1). Make four of these sets for each block. Join one set to the top and one to the bottom of each coloured square (Fig. 2). Sew a plain square to each end of the remaining two sets (Fig. 3), then join them to the sides of the coloured square to complete the star block. Make four yellow and five blue star blocks in the same way.

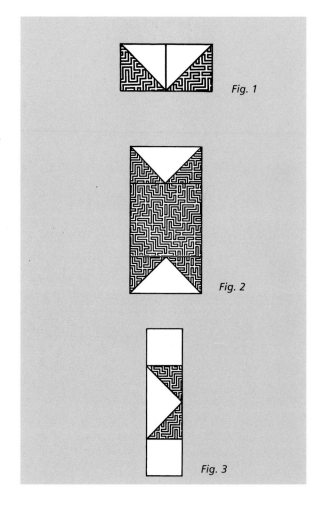

Fig. 1

Fig. 2

Fig. 3

CUTTING THE TWO-COLOUR SQUARES

ASSEMBLING

STEP ONE

Lay out the nine blocks in three rows of three blocks. Stitch them together, using a larger-than-normal stitch. Check that all the points meet accurately, then stitch over the seam again with a smaller stitch. This may look like 'double-handling', but it makes unpicking much easier, if it should be necessary.

STEP TWO

Stitch the side borders in place, then add the top and bottom borders.

HINT

This design will work equally well for many other simple geometric blocks. Decide on your chosen block, then draft it to the size you require on graph paper – a 6 cm (2 in) block works well. Glue the block onto a piece of firm cardboard, then cut it out. Cut the block into its components and use these as templates. Remember to add 7.5 mm (1/4 in) seam allowances when you cut them out of fabric.

TO FINISH

STEP ONE

Lay the backing face down. Centre the wadding on top and the quilt top on top of that, face upwards. Smooth out all the layers as you put them down, then pin them together, using the safety pins.

STEP TWO

Quilt as desired. Remember that miniatures require only minimal quilting as the main feature is the beautiful accurate piecing.

STEP THREE

Cut a 4 cm (1 1/2 in) wide bias strip of blue fabric. Press it over double with the wrong sides facing. Sew the binding to the top and bottom of the quilt with the raw edges matching. Sew the binding to the sides of the quilt, mitring the corners. Trim the seams. Fold the binding to the back and slipstitch it in place.

STEP FOUR

Make a sleeve for the back of the quilt, so you can hang it up. For instructions on how to make a hanging sleeve, see page 153.

STEP FIVE

Label your quilt.

ARRANGE ALL THE ELEMENTS FOR THE BLOCK

broderie perse needlecase

BY MARJORIE PATTERSON
Enjoy the challenge and the delightful effect you will achieve by appliquéing tiny chintz motifs onto a plain background in a technique known as broderie perse.

Broderie perse first appeared as an embroidery technique in the late sixteenth century when the complex process of printing cottons was mastered in India. These wonderful, bright, durable fabrics were brought to Europe and became the fashionable choice for clothing and furnishings. Chintz, as it became known, became highly prized and examples with floral designs featuring trailing tendrils and leaves were highly sought after. These pretty motifs could be cut out and stitched onto a background to make new and beautiful designs. Bedcovers made from chintz were highly desirable, but were very expensive. By using the motifs cut from small pieces of chintz and appliquéing them onto pastel fabrics, enterprising needlewomen were able to create cheaper versions of the furnishings they so desired. Often, the beautiful designs of the Indian palampores were copied using chintz cut-outs.

Broderie perse was also used in the centre of medallion quilts with borders of patchwork or appliqué. One of Australia's most significant quilts, the 'Rajah Quilt', made by convict women on their way to Australia, has a central square of broderie perse with more examples in the final border. Spectacular broderie perse quilts which took hundreds of hours of work and considerable skill, were made by women of wealth and leisure. Many of these quilts have survived.

Other items, such as tablecloths and napkins were decorated in the same way.

Initially, the fabrics used for broderie perse were of very good quality, but with the expansion of the fabric-printing industry, colour and design standards fell and the popularity of the technique declined. The *Dictionary of Needlecraft* of 1880 advised women to select their motifs from early chintz as the motifs had a distinct outline. After the introduction of aniline dyes, the designs were not so clearly delineated and were therefore less suitable to use.

This needlecase has been hand-pieced.

APPLIQUE AND EMBROIDERY PATTERN

FINISHED SIZE
7 cm x 9.5 cm (2³/4 in x 3³/4 in)

FABRIC REQUIREMENTS
20 cm x 30 cm (8 in x 12 in) of cream silk
10 cm x 15 cm (4 in x 6 in) of Pellon
Small piece of floral fabric with suitable motifs
10 cm x 12 cm (4 in x 4³/4 in) of felt

OTHER REQUIREMENTS
Stranded cotton for the twisted cord, one skein
  each of light and dark
Stranded cotton for the embroidery
Gold Charm bow, approximately 2.5 cm (1 in)
Embroidery needle
Rayon machine-embroidery thread or polycotton
  thread
Water-soluble marker pen
Small clear press stud
Pinking shears
Usual sewing supplies
Usual tracing and drawing supplies

CUTTING

STEP ONE

Cut the cream silk into two rectangles, each 10 cm x 15 cm (4 in x 6 in). Cut the felt into an 8 cm x 11.5 cm (3¼ in x 4½ in) using the pinking shears. Press the cream silk, Pellon and felt in half to mark the centres.

STEP TWO

From the floral fabric, cut out sixteen tiny flowers in various colours, leaving a seam allowance of approximately 3 mm (⅛ in) around each one.

APPLIQUE

See the appliqué and embroidery pattern on page 134.

STEP ONE

Using the water-soluble marker pen, trace the design for the floral spray and transfer it to the cream fabric so it is centred on one right-hand half. The best way to do this is to trace the design from page 134 directly onto the fabric. If this is not possible because your fabric is not sufficiently transparent, trace the design onto paper and go over the lines with a black marker pen. Place the tracing with the fabric on top on a light box, or a window with the light coming through it, and transfer the design.

STEP TWO

Using the rayon machine-embroidery thread or the polycotton thread, appliqué the tiny cut-out flowers into place. To do this, hold the flower in place with your left thumb and work in an anticlockwise direction, turning the seam allowance under with the needle as you go. For more information about hand-appliqué, see page 84.

GATHER ALL THE MATERIALS FOR THE PROJECT
BEFORE YOU BEGIN

CUT TINY FLOWER MOTIFS FROM FABRIC

THE COMBINATION OF APPLIQUE AND EMBROIDERY
CREATE A CHARMING EFFECT

EMBROIDERY

Using green stranded cotton, stem stitch the leaves and stems. Work bunches of French knots in the appropriate pastel colours. Attach the bow.

ASSEMBLING

STEP ONE

Using twelve 50 cm (20 in) strands each of the light and dark stranded cotton, make a twisted cord. Knot all the strands together at one end and secure this end to a door knob or hook. Twist the cords together, until they are well twisted, then take hold of them in the middle, allowing the two halves to twist around one another. Secure the loose ends.

STEP TWO

Place the two pieces of cream silk together with the right sides facing. Place the Pellon on top. Machine-stitch around the edges of the three layers in a 7.5 mm (1/4 in) seam, joining them together and leaving an opening in one side for turning. Trim the seams and turn through. Close the opening by hand.

TO FINISH

STEP ONE

Centre the felt inside the silk. Chain stitch it in place down the centre line.

STEP TWO

Using two strands of matching cotton, sew the twisted cord around the edge of the needlecase. Where the ends of the cord meet, make a tiny hole in the seam and poke the ends through. Close the opening by hand, as invisibly as you can.

STEP THREE

Attach the press stud so you can close the needlecase.

HINT

For broderie perse, choose elements from the printed fabric that have a clear outline that you can cut around easily. Use very sharp, small, pointed scissors for cutting to retain all the curves and points of the motif. Keep the size of the motifs in proportion to the area you are working on.

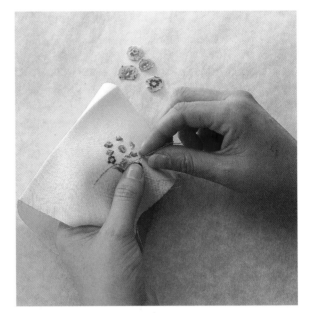

APPLIQUE THE SMALL FLOWERS ONTO THE SILK

CHAIN STITCH THE FELT INSIDE THE CASE

ring of shells cushion

**BY ANNIE LONDON
& SUSAN KAROLY**

This lovely cushion has been created using shadow trapunto which is an adaptation of a very old Italian technique.

The technique used involves stuffing a quilted design with wool to create the relief effect.

Antique examples of shadow trapunto incorporate areas, stuffed with cotton or wool in a neutral colour, to create the raised feature. These days, shadow trapunto has taken on a more contemporary, colourful look, and the stuffing and stitching are often coloured. Quite brightly coloured stuffing still produces a very soft appearance as it is filtered through white or cream batiste fabric. For this reason, it is advisable not to choose any coordinating fabrics, such as for the backing or ruffle, before the shadow trapunto is completed.

The cushion has been hand-quilted and finished by machine.

FINISHED SIZE

30 cm (12 in) square plus the ruffle

FABRIC REQUIREMENTS

Two 35 cm (14 in) squares of ivory polycotton batiste

35 cm (14 in) square of polyester wadding (split in half)

1 m (1³/4 yd) of pale blue cotton fabric for the back and the ruffle

OTHER REQUIREMENTS

Madeira Stranded Cotton, Coral Pink 813
Madeira Stranded Decora, White 1401
DMC Tapestry Wool: Pale Mushroom 7300, Pale Banana 7746, Pale Pink 7132, White, Pale Apricot 7853, Coral Pink 7852, Cream, Flesh 7191, Fawn 7164, Pale Turquoise 7587
Hand-quilting thread, Cream
Quilting needles, size 10
Tapestry needles, size 20
2 cm (³/4 in) wide masking tape
Tracing paper (optional)
Opalised seed beads, clear and blue
2 mm (¹/16 in) pearls
HB pencil
2 m (2¹/4 yd) of 23 mm (1 in) wide pink ribbon
Small quilting hoop
30 cm (12 in) cushion insert
Four shells

PREPARATION

See the pattern on page 141.

STEP ONE

Trace or photocopy the pattern. Tape the tracing or photocopy to a flat surface, using the masking tape.

STEP TWO

Fold one square of fabric into quarters and finger-press to mark the centre. Centre the square of fabric over the pattern and secure it with masking tape. Using the pencil, lightly trace the solid lines of the pattern and the crosses on the arms of the starfish. Do not trace the dotted line.

QUILTING
STEP ONE

Sandwich the wadding between the two squares of batiste fabric, with the traced pattern uppermost. Baste the layers together in grid fashion. Secure the fabric in the hoop.

STEP TWO

Using one strand of 813 cotton and the quilting needle, quilt the design, using small running stitches.

STEP THREE

Quilt the 2 cm (³/4 in) grid in the background of the design. The easiest way to mark this pattern is to use masking tape to indicate each line. When all the quilting is completed, remove the basting.

SHADOW TRAPUNTO
STEP ONE

Turn the piece over and lightly mark the dotted lines on the back. These lines indicate the colour changes which are indicated in the key on page 141. Thread a tapestry needle and, using the wool doubled, insert the needle through the back fabric and wadding, but not through the front fabric. Pull the needle through so the wool almost disappears into the fabric. Where the needle exits, cut the wool as close to the fabric as possible (Fig. 1).

ring of shells
cushion

Repeat this process as many times as is necessary to fill the area which is being coloured. The effect should be like a layer of cut, long stitches lying between the fabric and the wadding. Do not try to run a length of yarn that is longer than your needle – it is too hard to control. However, you can run the yarn in different directions to fill awkward spaces.

STEP TWO

After filling an area, there may be tiny ends of wool visible on the back. To tuck these inside, slide the needle under the back fabric, but not into the wadding, about 1 cm (½ in) from the wool end. Using the point of the needle, pull, hook or knock the ends inside (Fig. 2).

STEP THREE

Working from the right side of the piece, use the point of the needle to adjust the wool into any awkward parts of the design. Hold it up to the light to check if there are any gaps. If more stuffing is needed, turn the piece to the wrong side and add more yarn, as before.

STEP FOUR

Using one strand of Decora 1401, sew double-wrap French knots on the arms of the starfish where they are indicated on the pattern. Randomly stitch the beads and pearls in the blue sea areas.

TO FINISH

STEP ONE

Sew the pink ribbon around the quilted piece, folding it into neat mitres at the corners.

STEP TWO

Cut a 35 cm (14 in) square from the blue fabric for the cushion back. Cut 2.5 m (2¾ yd) of 15 cm wide strips from the blue fabric for the ruffle. Join the ends to make a loop. Press the seams open. Press the loop over double with the wrong sides together. Gather the raw edges of the loop. Pull up the gathering to fit around the edges of the cushion front. Pin the ruffle to the cushion front, adjusting the gathers and placing a little extra fullness at the corners. Stitch.

STEP THREE

With right sides together and the ruffle tucked out of the way, stitch the front to the back, leaving an opening. Turn the cushion to the right side. Slip the insert inside and close the opening by hand. Sew on some shells for the perfect finishing touch.

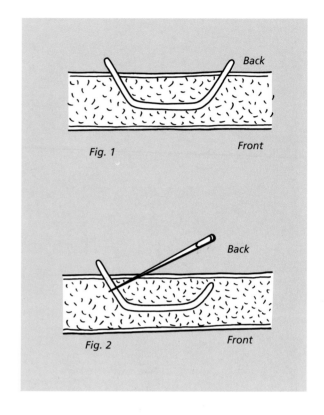

Fig. 1 — Back / Front

Fig. 2 — Back / Front

QUILTING THE DESIGN

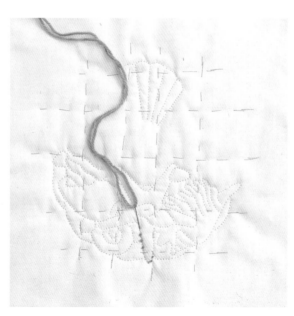

STUFFING THE DESIGN

CLOSE-UP OF SHADOW TRAPUNTO

KEY
a — 7300
b — 7746
c — 7132
d — White
e — 7853
f — 7852
g — Cream
h — 7191
i — 7164
j — 7587

PATTERN

BY EVELYN SEYMOUR

Patchwork made by the 'English' method has been popular since the beginning of the nineteenth century. This pretty tea cosy is easy to make using that lovely old technique.

In this technique, a template is made of metal or firm cardboard. Using this template, as many shapes are cut from light cardboard or paper as are required for the patchwork. The fabric is then cut out with a 7.5 mm (3/4 in) seam allowance added. The fabric is basted over the cardboard or paper, then the pieces are oversewn to join them. When all the patchwork is completed, the basting stitches are cut and the papers removed.

Wonderful quilts made by this method and using the shape most commonly associated with this method, the hexagon, have survived. Often a central shape was surrounded with six or more hexagons, creating a flower or rosette shape.

Many pieces of unfinished patchwork, complete with papers, also survive. The papers give us a wonderful glimpse into the lives of the women who covered them and also provide valuable assistance in dating these old pieces. Papers removed from old quilts have included fragments of letters, of a child's exercise book, old army papers and household accounts.

Although time-consuming, this method of patchwork gives the degree of accuracy prized by patchworkers. Despite the availability of sewing machines and quick-piecing methods, many still prefer the precision and portability that piecing over papers provides.

This lovely hexagon tea cosy gives you an opportunity to try this technique on a small scale. Using softly coloured fabrics reminiscent of the heyday of this type of patchwork, creating this tea cosy is quite a simple exercise, even for a beginner.

The method used for this type of patchwork today is still the same as that traditionally used, except that here template plastic has been used for the cutting template, instead of a metal one.

The hexagons have been hand-pieced and the tea cosy assembled by machine.

FINISHED SIZE

24 cm x 32 cm (9$\frac{1}{2}$ in x 12$\frac{1}{2}$ in)

FABRIC REQUIREMENTS

Scraps of brocades, silks, satins and cottons in soft shades

40 cm (16 in) square of Pellon

40 cm (16 in) of calico or homespun for the lining

OTHER REQUIREMENTS

Curtain ring
Perle 5 embroidery thread
Template plastic
Paper or thin cardboard
Matching sewing threads
Usual sewing supplies
Black fineline marker pen
Drawing and tracing materials

CUTTING

See the templates and the tea cosy pattern on page 145.

STEP ONE

Trace both hexagon templates onto the template plastic, using the marker pen and cut them out accurately, exactly on the marked line.

STEP TWO

Using the large hexagon template A, cut out 112 fabric hexagons from a variety of fabrics. These do not need to be absolutely accurate.

STEP THREE

Using the small hexagon template B, cut out 112 paper hexagons. These must be absolutely accurate if your pieces are to come together properly.

hexagon tea cosy

hexagon tea cosy

PIECING

STEP ONE

Centre a paper hexagon on the wrong side of each fabric hexagon. Fold one seam allowance over onto the paper, without folding or bending the paper, and baste it in place, stitching through the seam allowance and the paper. Fold the next adjacent seam allowance over, forming a crisp corner and baste it in the same way (Fig. 1). Work your way around each hexagon, until each is covered with basted fabric. It is a good idea not to secure the end of the basting threads as this allows for easy removal. Press all the hexagons gently.

STEP TWO

Place two hexagons together with the right sides facing. Begin about 7.5 mm (¼ in) from one corner of one matched edge and stitch to that corner, then stitch to the other end and work back for 7.5 mm (¼ in) again to secure the stitching (Fig. 2). Use a small whipstitch and matching sewing thread. You should have approximately sixteen stitches to 2.5 cm (1 in). Take care not to catch the papers in the seam; you should only be stitching through the fabric right on the edges and your stitches should be virtually invisible from the right side.

STEP THREE

Join the hexagons to make two pieces that are eight hexagons long and seven hexagons wide.

ASSEMBLING

STEP ONE

Trace the tea cosy pattern onto a piece of folded paper. Cut it out and unfold it to reveal the complete pattern. Using the pattern and allowing an additional 7.5 mm (¼ in) seam allowance, cut out two linings from calico, two shapes from Pellon and two from the pieced hexagons. Remove the papers from inside the hexagons.

STEP TWO

Join the two hexagon pieces, right sides facing, by stitching along the curved edge. Join the two calico pieces and the two Pellon pieces in the same way. On the Pellon only, cut back the seam allowance to 2 mm (¹⁄₁₆ in) and cut away the entire seam allowance from the bottom edges, to avoid bulk.

STEP THREE

Place the Pellon, then the calico, inside the hexagon tea cosy. Fold in the seam allowances of the hexagons and of the calico at the bottom edge. Slipstitch the folded edges together neatly.

TO FINISH

Make a tassel from the Perle thread. Using the same thread, buttonhole stitch around the curtain ring. Attach the tassel to the ring, then stitch both to the top of the tea cosy, catching the calico lining and the Pellon in the stitching, to hold them in place.

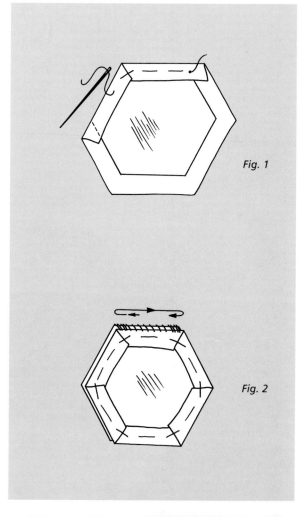

Fig. 1

Fig. 2

PIN THE HEXAGON FABRICS OVER PAPER

JOIN THE HEXAGONS WITH RIGHT SIDES FACING

CUT AND STITCH THE LINING

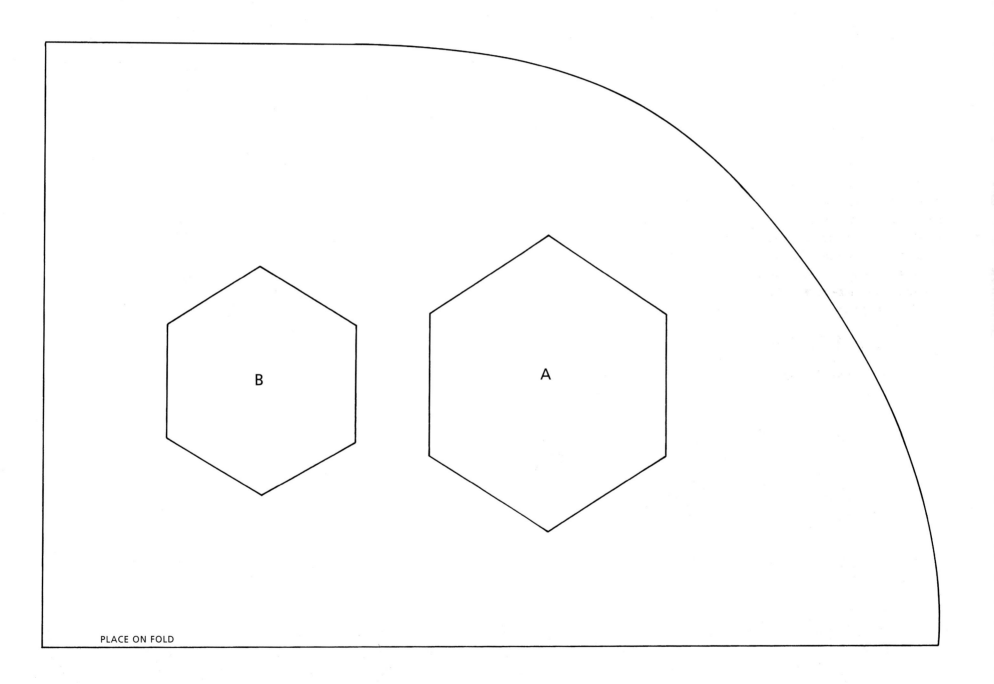

PLACE ON FOLD

B

A

TEMPLATES AND PATTERN

flying geese on foundation

BY VIRGINIA ENRIGHT

Foundation piecing is much admired for the accuracy it produces. This is particularly important if you are making a miniature quilt, such as this country-style 'Flying Geese' quilt.

Foundation piecing, as its name suggests, involves sewing the patches onto a piece of fabric, usually interfacing, which is the foundation. Calico and paper can also be used for the foundation, but paper is difficult to remove and calico is not as easy to work on.

This method allows even those with only basic sewing skills to create small, perfect quilts. It is similar to crazy patchwork, except that there is a formal pattern, rather than random piecing.

The important thing to remember is that you draw your pattern onto the foundation, then attach the patches on the unmarked side, so you are sewing along the marked lines. This method may take a little while to get comfortable with, but is really quite easy.

Begin by photocopying or tracing the pattern onto a sheet of white paper. This allows you to reuse the pattern a number of times. Tape the tracing to a firm surface. Place a piece of medium-weight interfacing over the pattern and trace the pattern onto it, using a sharp pencil. Remember, your finished piece can only be as accurate as the pattern you trace, so take your time and work carefully, using a ruler for the straight lines. Transfer the numbers on the pattern to the foundation – they indicate the order of sewing.

Adjust the stitch length on your sewing machine. Virginia's rule of thumb is 'the shorter the seam, the shorter the stitch length'.

The choice of fabric and design is as crucial to a miniature as to any quilt. Always include a variety of different-sized prints, as well as tone-on-tone fabrics. In this little quilt it is the tone-on-tone beige fabrics that form the background for the geese and add so much interest to the quilt. Spend some time sorting through your scrap basket to find just the right fabrics. Ask a friend for the leftover scraps from her favourite quilt. It's often a great challenge to work with unfamiliar fabrics.

This quilt is machine-pieced and machine-quilted with some hand-quilting in the borders.

FINISHED SIZE

Quilt: 35 cm x 41 cm (13¾ in x 16 in)

FABRIC REQUIREMENTS

Scraps of chosen fabrics for the 'geese'
Scraps of tone-on-tone beige fabrics for the background
5 cm (2 in) of green fabric for the sashing
15 cm (6 in) of fabric for the binding
45 cm x 51 cm (17¾ in x 20 in) of fabric for the backing
45 cm x 51 cm (17¾ in x 20 in) of wadding

OTHER REQUIREMENTS

Access to a photocopier or white paper for tracing
20 cm x 33 cm (8 in x 13 in) of medium-weight interfacing
Sewing thread in a neutral colour
Masking tape
Pencil or permanent marker pen
Rotary cutter
Quilter's ruler
Self-healing cutting mat
Hand-quilting thread (optional)
Hand-quilting needles (optional)
Usual sewing supplies
Spray starch
4 cm (1½ in) safety pins

PREPARING THE FOUNDATION

See the pattern on page 149. Note that it is given in two parts. You will need to join them when you trace or photocopy the pattern.

STEP ONE

Photocopy the pattern. If you don't have access to a photocopier, you can trace the pattern onto a sheet of white paper, using the marker pen. Tape the copy or tracing onto the work surface.

STEP TWO

Tape the interfacing over the pattern. Using the pencil or marker pen, carefully trace the pattern onto the interfacing three times. Transfer the numbers onto the interfacing; these indicate the order of sewing.

PIECING
STEP ONE

Cut the fabric scraps roughly into the sizes you will need – larger dark scraps and smaller beige scraps. To do this, look at the finished piece and cut a piece approximately that size plus seam allowances of 7.5 mm (1/4 in) plus a little extra. Err on the side of generosity when cutting out pieces. It is very frustrating to stitch a piece in place and flip it back – only to find it is too short. Be aware of the fabric grain when cutting out, but as the finished pieces will be supported by the foundation, you do not need to worry too much about bias edges stretching. For each pattern strip, cut ten large triangles from the dark prints and twenty small triangles from the beige scraps.

STEP TWO

Using one pattern strip and beginning with position 1, pin a large triangle to the unmarked side of the interfacing pattern, right side out. Hold the interfacing up to the light to check that the fabric piece is covering position 1 and that there is a sufficient overlap for the seam allowances on all sides.

STEP THREE

Pin the beige triangle 2 on the large triangle 1, with the right sides facing. Turn the interfacing over and sew on the line between 1 and 2. Begin the stitching three stitches before the line and end the stitching three stitches after the line. Trim the seam allowances and flip piece 2 over. Press or finger-press the seam, making sure there are no folds along the seam line. If you don't press accurately, you may lose some accuracy when the next piece is added.

STEP FOUR

Sew on beige triangle 3, in the same way, pinning it on the unmarked side of the interfacing and stitching along the line between 1 and 3 on the marked side. Trim the seam, flip the piece over and press.

STEP FIVE

Continue adding pieces in this way in the correct order. When the interfacing pattern is completely covered, the edges will look quite messy. Carefully press the strip then, using the rotary cutter, quilter's ruler and cutting mat,

trim the strip to 7.5 mm (1/4 in) outside the drawn line. Make three pieced strips of geese in the same way. Lay the three strips down on the work surface and determine the order in which you will join them

SASHING
STEP ONE

Cut two sashing strips, each 4 cm x 27 cm (1½ in x 10½ in). Sew a sashing strip to one of the pieced strips, with the right sides facing and sewing on the marked line on the interfacing as before. Flip the sashing over and press. Lay the 2.5 cm (1 in) mark of the ruler on the seam just sewn and trim the sashing, cutting along the edge of the ruler. This gives you a perfectly straight edge to attach to the next strip. Join the next pieced strip, another length of sashing, then another pieced strip to complete the centre of the quilt (Fig. 1).

STEP TWO

Cut two strips, each 4 cm x 27 cm (1½ in x 10½ in) from the sashing fabric. Sew these strips to the sides of the pieced centre.

STEP THREE

Cut two strips 4 cm x 21.5 cm (1½ in x 8½ in) from the sashing fabric. Sew these to the top and bottom of the pieced centre.

STEP FOUR

Trim these outer sashings in the same way as for the inner sashings. Lay the ruler with the 2.5 cm (1 in) mark on the seam and trim along the edge of the ruler.

BORDERS
STEP ONE

Cut two strips from the border fabric, each 9 cm x 31 cm (3½ in x 12 in). Sew them to the sides of the quilt.

STEP TWO

Cut two strips from the border fabric, each 9 cm x 36 cm (3½ in x 14 in). Sew them to the top and bottom of the quilt.

STEP THREE

Press and trim the borders as for the sashing, trimming them back to 7.5 cm (3 in) in width.

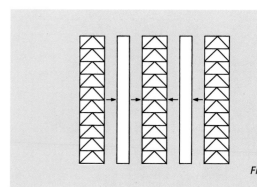

Fig. 1

ASSEMBLING
STEP ONE

Lay the backing face down on the ironing board with the wadding on top. Centre the pieced quilt top on top of that, face upwards. Gently press the three layers. This pressing helps to 'bond' the layers together and keep your finished piece flat.

STEP TWO

Pin the three layers together, then baste or pin-baste in the usual way.

QUILTING

Quilt 'in-the-ditch' around the pieced strips, borders and sashing. Virginia has hand-quilted the borders, using a commercial stencil.

TO FINISH
STEP ONE

Cut the binding 4.5 cm (1¾ in) wide on the straight grain of the fabric. Press the binding strips over double with the wrong sides facing. Pin, then stitch the binding to the sides of the quilt, on the right side and with the raw edges even. Turn the folded edge to the back of the quilt and slipstitch it in place. Bind the top and the bottom in the same way, allowing 1.25 cm (½ in) at the ends for turning under.

STEP TWO

If your miniature is to be hung, make a sleeve for the back, following the instructions on page 153.

STEP THREE

Label your quilt.

CLOSE-UP OF THE PIECING

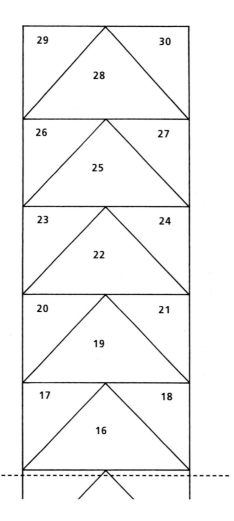

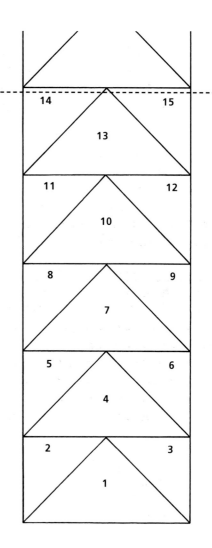

FOUNDATION PATTERN
NOTE THE PATTERN IS GIVEN IN TWO PARTS. TRACE OR PHOTOCOPY THEM AS A SINGLE UNIT

FABRIC
CHOOSING FABRIC

Colour is the single most significant element of a quilt, followed by pattern and execution. The most skilfully made and intricately designed quilt will fail if the colour choices are poor.

Choosing the fabrics is often the most daunting element of beginning a quilt. We all know what colours we like, but we are not all so certain of what colours will work together to create the effect we are seeking. Take the time to explore the fabrics in your local patchwork shop and to enlist the help of the staff.

These days a staggering variety of patchwork fabrics is available in department stores and specialist patchwork shops. This very fact can make choosing difficult. Start with one fabric that appeals to you, then look for the fabrics which work well with it. Make sure you choose fabrics with sufficient contrast otherwise the finished quilt can look very bland.

Choose one hundred per cent cotton fabrics. They are much easier to work with than polyester or blended fabrics. Sometimes, the perfect colour or texture you need for your quilt can only be found in a polyester fabric, such as in 'In the Red' on page 64. The quiltmaker felt the lamé fabric was essential and was prepared to struggle with the consequences. There are things you can do, such as stabilising the fabric with light interfacing, so if you must have that shiny silk or plush velvet – go for it!

PREPARING FABRIC

Many quiltmakers prefer to wash all the fabrics for a quilt before they begin, to ensure they are colourfast and to remove any chemical size from the fabric. Others, generally those who can't wait to begin, just hop right in and begin cutting.

If there is any fabric whose fastness is suspect, generally these are the deep reds, blues and purples, test it first. Cut off a small scrap and soak it in warm water. If no colour bleeds, it's probably fine. If colour does bleed, see if washing it in warm, soapy water, then rinsing until the water runs clear stops the bleeding. Soaking it in white vinegar can sometimes set the dye. If it doesn't work, do not use the fabric. Imagine if you wash your newly completed quilt, only to have the dye run and spoil it completely.

Press the fabrics while they are still slightly damp.

KNOW YOUR FABRIC

It is important to recognise the features of a piece of fabric, before you begin cutting. The lengthwise grain is the most stable (least likely to stretch) and runs down the length of the fabric. The crosswise grain follows the weave of the fabric across the width. The bias is the diagonal across the fabric which is formed when the lengthwise and crosswise grains are matching. This is the stretchiest grain of the fabric and is very useful if you want to curve the fabric, such as for appliqué flower stems. It is important to respect the grain of the fabric when you are cutting pieces for a quilt, if you want them to retain their shape and come together properly.

Templates for hand-piecing generally have the grain line marked on them. Match this line to the fabric grain, crosswise or lengthwise.

CUTTING AND PIECING

Separate instructions are given for cutting and hand-piecing (pages 8–9) and cutting and machine-piecing (page 48). Refer to these instructions before proceeding.

BORDERS

Borders are used to frame a quilt top, or to increase its size. They can be narrow or wide, pieced or plain – whatever best suits the quilt top. Some quilts look great with no border at all.

For the border, choose fabrics that reflect the 'feel' of the quilt; either a new fabric to complement what has already been completed or a fabric already in the pieced top. To select your border fabric, lay the fabric around the edge of the quilt top to see if it 'works'.

Pieced borders can add an additional dimension to the quilt, but many less-experienced quilters are daunted by the job of working out how many pieced units are required to fit the size of the quilt. Divide the length of the border by the length of the pieced unit. This should give you the number of pieced units required but, unfortunately, it is often not accurate. Tiny variations in cutting and sewing can throw this calculation out. Adding another narrow strip between the quilt top and pieced border can fill the gap. Enlarging the seam allowances on the pieced strip to make it shorter, while still retaining the same number of units, can also fix the problem. Experiment and don't be discouraged!

Finish one border before you attach the next one. The exception to this rule would be if you are attaching a number of plain borders and intend to mitre the corners. Many quiltmakers join these together before attaching them to the quilt and mitring the corners.

The instructions in this book give suggested measurements for borders, but it is always best to measure your own pieced top to be sure. Don't just attach a border, thinking you'll trim it to size later. You won't end up with a square quilt. Measure the finished pieced top across the middle, vertically and horizontally, to give the quilt size. Remember, one of these measurements must include double the width of the border. Cut the borders in one length, with no joins.

BORDERS WITH SQUARE CORNERS

For width, cut border strips the width of the quilt plus seam allowances (Fig. 1). For length, cut border strips the length of the quilt plus twice the width of the border strip plus seam allowances of 7.5 mm (^{1}/4 in) (Fig. 2). Pin and sew the side borders to the quilt top, matching centres and ends. Pin and sew the top and bottom borders to the quilt top in the same way. Sew with the border strips on top. Press the border over the stitching line. Which way you press the border may depend on the colour of the quilt top and of the border, or on the quilting pattern.

BORDERS WITH MITRED CORNERS

For length or width, cut the border strips the length or width of the quilt top plus twice the width of the border strip plus an extra 10 cm (4 in) allowance. Find the centre of each strip and the centre of the edge of the quilt by folding. Sew the border strips to two sides of the quilt top with the right sides together, matching centres. Begin and end the stitching 7.5 mm (^{1}/4 in) from the corners of the pieced top. The excess border fabric will extend beyond the edge of the quilt top, equally at both ends. Sew the remaining border strips to the other two sides of the quilt in the same manner, making sure that the seam stops at the same place as the previous seam. Press.

On the wrong side, fold the border strips back at an angle of forty-five degrees so that they touch one another, then finger-press the fold (Fig. 3). Matching the creases and stitching exactly on them, beginning from the outside, stitch the mitres. Trim off the excess seam allowance. Press the seam open.

PREPARATION FOR QUILTING
THE BACKING

Cut the backing at least 10 cm (4 in) larger all around than the quilt top. You may need to sew two or three lengths of fabric together to make the backing reach the required size. Trim the selvages off the fabric, before cutting and rejoining lengths. Press these seams open to assist in quilting.

Consider using an interesting pieced backing if you need to enlarge the size. On the other hand, some quiltmakers use the opportunity to join together a few 'orphan' fabrics in a fairly haphazard way. A pieced backing is a wonderful surprise to discover when you turn a quilt over.

If your quilt has a lot of pale fabrics, take care to choose a light-coloured backing fabric, to prevent the backing showing through. Print fabrics are great for backing as they are less revealing of quilting errors than a plain fabric.

THE WADDING (BATTING)

Wadding can be purchased in various weights, widths and fibre content. For hand-quilting, low-loft polyester wadding is best. For machine-quilting, low-loft polyester wadding or cotton wadding is suitable. Cotton wadding may need to be pre-shrunk; check the manufacturer's instructions. Some quiltmakers favour the look of cotton wadding because it gives their quilts a genuine antique look and feel.

Cut the wadding slightly smaller than the backing and a little larger than the quilt top. If your piece of wadding is not big enough, then it may be pieced. Do not overlap pieces of wadding when joining them, just butt pieces together and join them with a zigzag stitch that catches both pieces.

THE QUILT SANDWICH

Place the backing face down on the floor or on a large table, such as a table tennis table. Use masking tape or large safety pins (in the case of carpet) to secure the backing. Make sure the fabric is as smooth as it can be and the corners are square. Centre the wadding on the backing and smooth it out. Next comes the quilt top, face up in the centre, with its edges parallel to the backing edges. Smooth the quilt top gently to remove any wrinkles (Fig. 4).

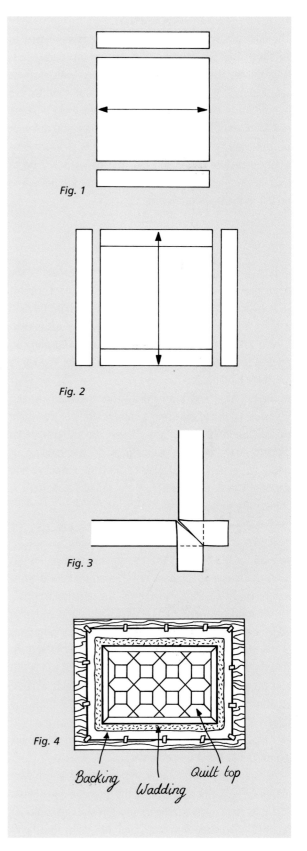

Fig. 1

Fig. 2

Fig. 3

Fig. 4

Backing Wadding Quilt top

BASTING

The quilt sandwich can be secured with rows of basting stitches; this is described in detail on page 151. Alternatively the quilt may be pin-basted with stainless safety pins (Fig. 5). You will need about four to five hundred pins to baste a double-bed quilt. Place a safety pin approximately every 10 cm (4 in). When you put your outstretched hand on the quilt, you should touch four safety pins. The closer you pin, the easier it will be to quilt. Take care to choose rustless safety pins if they are to be left in the quilt for a while.

BINDING

Almost the last step in the quiltmaking process is the binding and it is very important to get it right. For most straight-edge quilts, 9 cm (3½ in) wide straight binding is used, folded over double, lengthwise. For quilts with curved edges, such as the '1920s Floral Appliqué' on page 120, use bias strips. Miniature quilts require a narrower binding.

Before attaching the binding, trim the wadding and the backing. If you are using a narrow binding, trim them to the size of the quilt top. If you are using a wider binding, leave enough wadding to fill the binding. A rotary cutter is the best way to trim the wadding and backing. Check that the edges are straight and that the corners are square.

Prepare binding strips the length and width of the quilt plus 2.5 cm (1 in), checking the measurements as you did for the borders. The measurements given in this book include an additional 4 cm (1½ in) for adjustments. Join pieces, if necessary, to achieve the required length.

Working on the right side of the quilt and with raw edges matching, stitch the binding to the two long sides of the quilt. Turn the folded edge to the back of the quilt. Trim the seam, then attach the remaining strips to the top and bottom of the quilt, making sure there is at least 12 mm (½ in) excess binding at each end. Turn the folded edge of the binding over to the back of the quilt and slipstitch all the binding in place, folding the excess length to cover the raw edges.

Bias binding is often attached in a single length with mitred corners. Measure around the quilt and add at least 15 cm (6 in) to allow for the mitred corners. Cut sufficient 9 cm (3½ in) wide bias strips and join them to achieve the required length. Try to avoid placing joining seams at the corners as the bulk can be difficult to handle.

Start the binding near the centre of one of the sides of the quilt. Leave the first 5 cm (2 in) loose to overlap later. When you reach the corner, stop the stitching 1 cm (³/8 in) from the edge and back stitch. Cut the thread and remove the quilt from the machine. Lay the quilt on a flat surface and fold the binding up and away from the quilt (Fig. 6) then fold it again so that it lies along the next edge of the quilt to be sewn (Fig. 7). Start stitching from the fold in the binding to the next corner and repeat. When you reach the starting point, overlap the bindings at an angle of forty-five degrees and slipstitch. Turn the binding to the back of the quilt, and slipstitch it in place. At the corners, fold the binding to form mitres on both the front and back of the quilt and stitch it down (Fig. 8).

CONTINUOUS BIAS BINDING

For longer lengths of bias binding, cut continuous bias. A 115 cm (45 in) square of fabric will yield approximately 18 m (20 yd) of 4 cm (1½ in) wide bias strip.

Cut a square of fabric, then cut it in half, diagonally. With the right sides facing, join two of the short sides in a 7.5 mm (¼ in) seam (Fig. 9). Press the seam open, then trim to 3 mm (⅛ in).

On the back of the fabric, mark parallel lines 4 cm (1½ in) apart (Fig. 10).

With the right sides facing, bring the edges together so that the top edge on one side matches the first marked line on the other side. Stitch a 7.5 mm (¼ in) seam (Fig. 11). Trim the seam allowance to 3 mm (⅛ in). Press the seam open. Cut the bias strip in a continuous spiral, cutting along the marked lines (Fig. 12).

LABELLING YOUR QUILT

It is essential that you sign and date your work at the very least. But so many lovely old quilts give us no information about them that it would be good to include who the quilt was made for and why, the name of the quilt, where you come from and anything else interesting for future generations. You can type or write on fabric if you iron a piece of plastic-coated freezer paper to it first. Test a sample to be absolutely sure that the ink is permanent. Sew the completed label to the back of the quilt. Alternatively, you can embroider your label, or simply handwrite it using a permanent marking pen.

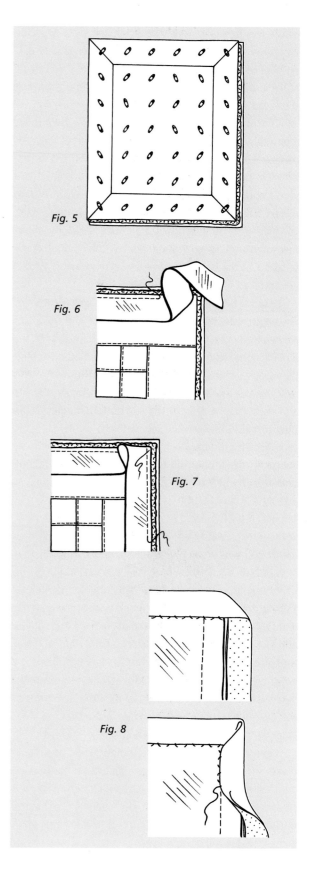

Fig. 5

Fig. 6

Fig. 7

Fig. 8

HANGING SLEEVE

For quilts which are meant to be hung rather than laid on a bed, a tube of fabric, called a hanging sleeve, must be attached to the back.

Cut a 22 cm (8¾ in) wide strip of fabric that is the width of the quilt. Sew a 7.5 mm (¼ in) double hem on the short ends. Fold the strip over double, lengthwise, with the wrong sides facing. Sew a 1 cm (³/8 in) seam along the long side (Fig. 13). Press the seam open and roll it around so the seam is at the back (Fig. 14). Pin the top of the sleeve just under the top of the quilt and slipstitch it in place. Roll the sleeve up so it is level with the top of the quilt and slipstitch the bottom of the sleeve to the quilt (Fig. 15).

CARE OF QUILTS

If you have pre-washed your fabrics, your quilt can be washed on a gentle cycle with very mild detergent and tumble-dried on a cool setting. You may hang the quilt in the shade to dry or lay it out flat in a shady place, if you wish. Take the quilt indoors as soon as it is thoroughly dry. Inside the home, keep quilts out of direct sunlight and fluorescent light.

To store your quilt, fold it and place it in a one hundred per cent cotton pillowcase or an acid-free box. Do not store it in plastic. Refold the quilt occasionally so that ridges do not form.

MEASUREMENTS

There are both imperial and metric measurements given throughout this book. These are not exact conversions. The measurements have been adjusted as necessary to ensure that the quilt goes together well. In cases where the conversion is less critical, such as for fabric quantities, the measurements have been rounded out for ease of working. However, the two sets of figures are not interchangeable. It is important that you work only in one form of measurement for any one quilt – imperial or metric – and don't switch between them.

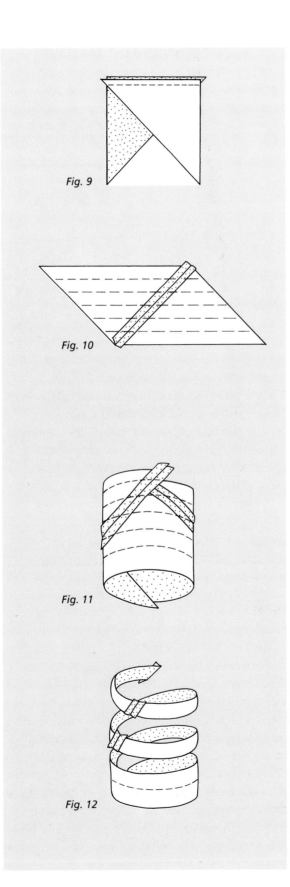

Fig. 9

Fig. 10

Fig. 11

Fig. 12

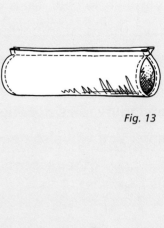

Fig. 13

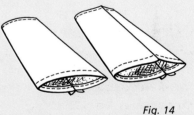

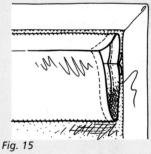

Fig. 14

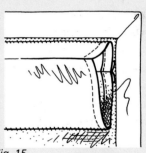

Fig. 15

tools of
the trade

If you like to sew, then you will already have the most important tools you will need to make the quilts in this book – a sewing machine or hand-sewing needles, sewing thread and scissors. You will also need a few other essential tools.

CUTTING EQUIPMENT

A rotary cutter and a self-healing cutting mat are great aids for quick cutting. The rotary cutter looks like a round pizza cutter. It has a shield over the blade which must be respected because it is very sharp. Pull back the shield when you cut the fabric and push it back into place immediately you are finished. The special cutting mat also protects the blade on your cutter from damage. With a dull spot on the blade, you will never cut beautiful straight strips – they will always look ragged – so change the blade as soon as it starts to become dull.

RULERS

There are many rulers available, but one is particularly suitable for quilting. It is approximately 61 cm x 15 cm (24 in x 6 in). This extra width is an advantage and there are also 45-degree and 60-degree angles marked on it. The edges of the ruler are thick enough to allow you to cut accurately with your rotary cutter.

SCISSORS

You will need good scissors for cutting fabric and some less precious ones to cut paper and template plastic. A pair of small snips for cutting threads would also be handy to have at hand.

THREAD

Always use good thread for quilting. Do not try to economise with cheap thread. Your quilt is going to last years and years and it would be very sad to lose all your hard work by having the threads break. If you are going to sew by hand, it is even more important to buy good thread. Quality threads will save you endless time because they will not constantly shred.

For hand-piecing and appliqué, a number 50 cotton thread is very good. Polyester threads are not suitable, as they are stronger than the fabric that is being sewn and they could eventually cut through the quilt. Cotton-covered polyester threads are a good compromise.

For hand-quilting, use cotton quilting thread. Thread it through the needle as it comes off the spool. This way you will be sewing with the natural twist of the thread which is less likely to knot.

You won't need a huge range of colours. Some quiltmakers use a neutral-coloured thread for all their piecing – cream or beige is fine for light-coloured fabrics and a dark grey/green thread for dark fabrics.

Old thread dries out, so don't store it for years. Sometimes you can reclaim old thread by putting it in the refrigerator in a paper bag for a while.

Monofilament, or invisible, thread is great for quilting. Use it in the needle of your machine and a cotton or polycotton thread to match the quilt back in the bobbin.

SEWING MACHINE

Be kind to your sewing machine and look after it; it will repay you by lasting well and giving good service for a very long time. Replace the needle often, especially after machine-quilting. Use a number 80 needle for all your machine-piecing and machine-quilting.

Sewing through the quilt 'sandwich' is hard on a sewing machine so give it a treat: brush out the fluff, and oil the machine before you put it away or, if you haven't done it recently, before you use it next time.

Have your machine serviced regularly, especially if you are having problems with the tension. Don't thread the bobbin with thread on top of another thread just to avoid waste. You will never find the old thread when you want it anyway! Buy some extra bobbins to have ready when you change thread colours.

HAND-SEWING NEEDLES

Size 8 or 9 betweens needles are fine for hand-sewing and hand-appliqué. For hand-quilting, most quilters use a size 9 or 10 quilting needle. Very good hand-quilters usually recommend number 12 needles. Buy a pack of mixed quilting needles and experiment to find out which one works for you. Generally, the finer the needle, the smaller the stitch.

For basting, use a long thin sewing needle which allows you to take many stitches at one time. Some quiltmakers use a doll needle, which is especially long, for basting their quilts.

PINS

If you have to pin, plastic-headed or glass-headed pins are best. They are bigger and can be seen more easily when you are sewing. Most quick-sewing methods do not require pinning, but appliqué usually does.

Safety pins, approximately 4 cm (1¹/₂ in) long are often used for securing the layers of the quilt 'sandwich', instead of basting. Check the points of your safety pins to ensure they are not rough or blunt, or they will pluck threads in your quilt top. A small piece of sandpaper will help smooth the point – or just throw out the blunt ones. You will need approximately four to five hundred pins for a double bed quilt and these can often be bought in bulk from your local quilt shop.

TEMPLATE PLASTIC

Template plastic is a sheet of clear or nearly clear plastic that allows you to see through it and to trace patterns directly onto it. The plastic also needs to be clear enough so that you can place the template on the correct line or pattern on the fabric, especially when you are using striped fabric. In the past, cardboard was used for templates but the edges very soon became ragged, so these days plastic is preferred. You can draw on template plastic with a permanent marker pen.

PENCILS AND PENS

Marker pens and pencils for marking are available at your local quilt shop or you can buy a soft lead pencil from the newsagent. A fabric eraser can be used to remove pencil marks from your quilt top.

Water-soluble fabric marker pens are also available, but always be sure to test that a particular pen will come off your fabric before you use it on your quilt top. Wash the pen marks out under a running tap, don't just spray them with a water bottle or just touch them with a damp cloth. If the mark is not completely removed, it may come back to mark your quilt at a later date.

Yellow and silver pencils are used for marking darker fabrics. For marking for hand-quilting, you can use a soft pencil or even the tailor's chalk pencils that are available in the haberdashery stores. These are not suitable for machine-quilting because the marks come off too easily with handling. Light pencil marks will usually wear off or wash off quite easily.

HOOPS AND FRAMES

Quilter's hoops and frames hold the quilt with an even tension while you quilt, and define the quilt area. There are several types on the market: square polyurethane frames, round wooden frames and floor frames. Start with a reasonably sized hoop or frame and try it out. Better still, if you can borrow one from a friend, try it before you buy to see if this is the one for you. A hoop or frame is not necessary for machine-quilting, but is essential for hand-quilting.

THIMBLES

Thimbles are a must for hand-quilters and are commonly used on the third finger of the upper hand. If you are not used to wearing a thimble, it will feel awkward at first, but persevere. It is essential if you are going to push the needle through the layers of the quilt. Some quilters also wear a leather one for the hand underneath the quilt. Try a variety of thimbles until you find some to suit you.

SOME OF THE EQUIPMENT YOU MIGHT NEED IS PICTURED BELOW

Published by
SALLY MILNER PUBLISHING PTY LTD
PO Box 2104
BOWRAL   NSW   2576
AUSTRALIA
www.sallymilner.com.au

Printed by TOPPAN PRINTING CO., HONG KONG

© Sally Milner Publishing Pty Ltd 2001

National Library of Australia Cataloguing-in-Publication data:
The handbook of quilting.

   ISBN 1 86351 280 2.

   1. Quilting. 2. Quilting - Patterns. I. Poulos,
    Judy.
   (Series: Milner craft series).

   746.46

Disclaimer
The information in this instruction book is
presented in good faith. However, no warranty is
given, nor results guaranteed, nor is freedom from
any patent to be inferred. Since we have no
control over the use of information contained in
this book, the publisher and the author disclaim
liability for untoward results.

EDITORIAL

MANAGING EDITOR
Judy Poulos
CONTRIBUTING EDITORS
Karen Fail, Kate McEwen

PHOTOGRAPHY
Andrew Payne, Andrew Elton

STYLING
Louise Owens, Kathy Tripp

ILLUSTRATION
Lesley Griffith, Maggie Cooper

PRODUCTION AND DESIGN

PRODUCTION DIRECTOR
Anna Maguire
DESIGN MANAGER
Drew Buckmaster
PRODUCTION COORDINATOR
Meredith Johnson
PRODUCTION ARTISTS
Petra Rode, Lulu Dougherty
JUNIOR PRODUCTION EDITOR
Heather Straton